CONSTELLATIONS

Like the future itself, the imaginative possibilities of science fiction are limitless. And the very development of cinema is inextricably linked to the genre, which, from the earliest depictions of space travel and the robots of silent cinema to the immersive 3D wonders of contemporary blockbusters, has continually pushed at the boundaries. **Constellations** provides a unique opportunity for writers to share their passion for science fiction cinema in a book-length format, each title devoted to a significant film from the genre. Writers place their chosen film in a variety of contexts – generic, institutional, social, historical – enabling **Constellations** to map the terrain of science fiction cinema from the past to the present... and the future.

'This stunning, sharp series of books fills a real need for authoritative, compact studies of key science fiction films. Written in a direct and accessible style by some of the top critics in the field, brilliantly designed, lavishly illustrated and set in a very modern typeface that really shows off the text to best advantage, the volumes in the **Constellations** series promise to set the standard for SF film studies in the 21st century.'
Wheeler Winston Dixon, Ryan Professor of Film Studies, University of Nebraska

 Constellations

Constelbooks

Also available in this series

Blade Runner Sean Redmond

Children of Men Dan Dinello

Close Encounters of the Third Kind Jon Towlson

The Damned Nick Riddle

Dune Christian McCrea

Inception David Carter

RoboCop Omar Ahmed

Rollerball Andrew Nette

Forthcoming

Brainstorm Joseph Maddrey

Ex Machina Joshua Grimm

Jurassic Park Paul Bullock

Mad Max Martyn Conterio

Stalker Jon Hoel

CONSTELLATIONS

12 Monkeys

Susanne Kord

First published in 2019 by
Auteur, 24 Hartwell Crescent, Leighton Buzzard LU7 1NP
www.auteur.co.uk
Copyright © Auteur 2019

Series design: Nikki Hamlett at Cassels Design
Set by Cassels Design www.casselsdesign.co.uk
Printed and bound in Great Britain

British Library Cataloguing-in-Publication Data
A catalogue record for this book is available from the British Library

ISBN paperback: 978-1-9993340-0-0
ISBN ebook: 978-1-9993340-1-7

Contents

Dedication

To John, my travelling companion through time and space

I. 'A Spectacular Mess': Synopsis

12 Monkeys (1995) was written by David Peoples, co-author of *Blade Runner* (1982, dir. Ridley Scott) and author of *Unforgiven* (1992, dir. Clint Eastwood), and his wife and collaborator Janet Peoples. Directed by Terry Gilliam of *Monty Python* fame (figure 1), the film was made on an extremely modest budget of slightly under $30 million.[1] As a result, the film's stars were required to work for far less than their usual fee, and the film was subjected to cuts on sets and an abbreviated shooting schedule. Gilliam famously described the process as 'the most unenjoyable filmmaking experience I've ever had'.[2] Given its less-than-ideal inception, the film nevertheless defied expectations, not least Terry Gilliam's, by raking in $170 million worldwide and receiving a number of nominations and awards. Together with *The Fisher King* (1991), it is still Gilliam's most commercially successful film.

Figure 1: Terry Gilliam shooting 12 Monkeys

Critics, however, have not been as uniformly enthusiastic as audiences. *12 Monkeys* has been called 'a spectacular mess, a convoluted film with too many ideas for its own good',[3] a film with 'an involving, occasionally baffling storyline',[4] 'a narrative which descends into a morass of Hollywood thriller clichés and conventions',[5] or simply 'overwrought, messy, and confusing'.[6] Small wonder, then, that baffled scholars have turned to the world's greatest minds to help them solve Gilliam's riddle. By now, the full intellectual force of Sigmund Freud, Mikhail Bakhtin, Martin

Heidegger, Gilles Deleuze, Michel Foucault and Friedrich Nietzsche have been brought to bear on the film.[7]

The degree to which critics and bloggers have disagreed even on plot fundamentals is startling, and this, too, has been pointed out repeatedly. The film 'precipitated an infinite regress of heated speculation by the public and film scholars alike', writes Greenberg. 'Whether deliberately or unintentionally the screenplay leaves many points obscure. At least several of its reiterated givens are in fact highly debatable [...], arguably even escaping the conscious intentions of its creators.'[8] I would quibble with Greenberg's implication that the screenwriters and director do not understand their own film (and intend to show otherwise in chapters 3-7), but I agree that even the simplest of all questions about *12 Monkeys*, i.e. what happens in it, has generated a great deal of bewilderment. The synopsis I offer below limits itself to those plot strands that are largely uncontested:[9]

The year is 2035, the place a ruined and abandoned Philadelphia. Following the extinction of 99 per cent of the human race by a deadly virus released deliberately in 1996, the surviving one per cent lead a miserable subterranean existence because the Earth's surface, while still accommodating to animals who roam it freely, has become uninhabitable for humans. Surviving humanity is marked by a tyrannical social hierarchy in which a caste of scientists, who study the virus in an attempt to develop a serum that would enable them to repopulate the Earth's surface, rule with an iron fist over everyone else, their test subjects. These subjects are caged like animals, severely punished at the slightest disobedience, and forced to 'volunteer' for scientific experiments and dangerous missions from which few ever return. When a distorted phone message from the past names a group known as the Army of the Twelve Monkeys as the originators of the deadly virus, the scientists send James Cole (Bruce Willis), a prisoner serving 25 years to life for 'insolence, defiance, disregard of authority', back to 1996 to find the original virus, because only the virus in its primary and unmutated form will serve as the basis for an effective serum. While Cole's main qualification, as he is repeatedly told, is that he is 'a good observer' and 'tough-minded' (meaning mentally strong enough to withstand repeated time-travel), Cole is something of a tortured soul. He is vulnerable, mistreated, despondent, disoriented and plagued by a recurring nightmare in which a young boy, easily identifiable as

Cole himself, witnesses the shooting of a man at an airport.

A miscalculation on the scientists' part lands Cole not, as envisioned, in 1996 but in 1990, where further 'defiance' of his arresting officers and his ravings about the end of the world promptly land him in a lunatic asylum. The examining psychiatrist, Dr. Kathryn Railly (Madeleine Stowe), expresses the feeling that she has seen him before. In the mental hospital Cole encounters Jeffrey Goines (Brad Pitt), a patient who helps him escape. Promptly recaptured, Cole is sedated and locked in a cell, from where the scientists yank him back to 2035. The scientists have meanwhile partially decoded the distorted voicemail message pointing to the Army of the Twelve Monkeys as the originators of the virus, which they play to Cole, also showing him pictures of several other suspects, which appear to include Jeffrey Goines. After Cole explains that they sent him to the wrong year, where he was imprisoned and drugged, the scientists promise to send him back to the correct year this time—the third quarter of 1996, 'right on the money'. Instead, he lands in a World War I trench. There he briefly encounters his next-cell neighbour Jose (Jon Seda), who has also been transported there in error. Cole is shot in the leg and then suddenly, if belatedly, propelled to the correct time.

As Cole, now wounded, finally lands in 1996, Railly is giving a lecture about the Cassandra complex to a group of scientists. At the post-lecture book signing, a Dr. Peters (David Morse) tells a distracted and barely listening Railly that 'Chicken Little represents the sane vision', and that apocalypse alarmists are quite correct in claiming that humanity's destruction of the environment will lead to the end of the world. Cole kidnaps Railly after the lecture and forces her to take him to Philadelphia, where they identify Jeffrey Goines as the founder and leader of the Army of the Twelve Monkeys. That this group is responsible for viral Armageddon is strongly indicated by the fact that Goines' millionaire father Leland Goines (Christopher Plummer) is a famous virologist, that the deadly virus is being developed in his laboratory, and that Jeffrey Goines has been working for his father since his release from the asylum. But when Cole confronts Jeffrey at a black-tie dinner held at the Goines mansion, Jeffrey denies any involvement with the group and claims that Cole himself planted the idea of wiping out humanity in his mind during their 1990 encounter in the mental hospital.

Transported back to 2035, Cole, now secretly convinced that he is insane, manages to persuade the suspicious scientists that he intends to complete his mission. Once returned to 1996, however, he tells Railly that he is not from the future, that there is no such thing as time travel, that the world is not ending, and that he needs help to get well. Railly, who has up to this point desperately tried to convince him of this very thing, conversely now believes his earlier ravings about time travel and the end of the world. Incontrovertible evidence indicating this include a photograph in her own book showing Cole in a World War I trench, and the fact that the bullet she herself removed from Cole's leg turns out to have been cast before 1920. As Cole basks in the blissful illusion that he is insane, which means that he can live out his life in the glorious past full of what he considers clean air and wonderful music, the horrifying truth dawns on Railly: if Cole is a time traveller, it means the End is Nigh.

Together they find the Army Headquarters of the Twelve Monkeys behind a shabby storefront in Philadelphia, then decide, assuming imminent Armageddon, to travel to the Florida Keys to fulfil Cole's long-held dream of seeing the sea. Railly leaves a phone message for the scientists of the future pointing to the Twelve Monkeys as the guilty party, the message which, badly distorted, started (will start) the scientists' investigation. But when the Army, instead of releasing the deadly virus, frees animals from the zoo and locks Leland Goines in an animal cage, Railly and Cole become convinced that the Twelve Monkeys are a bunch of harmless hippie activists rather than the source of the virus. They disguise themselves—he with a Hawaiian tourist shirt, straw hat, fake hair and moustache; she with a blonde wig—at a showing of Alfred Hitchcock's *Vertigo* (1958). Cole claims he recognises lines from the *Vertigo* scene in which Kim Novak's character traces the short years of her previous life on the rings of a felled Sequoia tree, and both Cole and Railly recognise each other in their respective disguises, although they're seeing each other dressed in this manner for the first time.

Ignoring all of these warning signs, they proceed to the airport, where Cole is again beset by an uncanny feeling that he has been there before. He leaves a final phone message for the scientists, telling them that the Twelve Monkeys group is not responsible, that he doesn't know who is, that he considers his mission fulfilled, and that he will not return to the future. As he hangs up, Jose appears, handing him a gun and instructing him to follow orders: the scientists of the future have taken thirty years to decode the message Cole has just left and sent Jose in response. At the same time, Railly spots Dr. Peters, recognising him simultaneously as the apocalypse nut at her lecture and from a photograph showing him at Leland Goines' virology lab, and instantly concludes that it is he who is about to release the virus. Indeed, Peters is about to take the virus on a tour around the globe, with stops at several major cities. Railly points Peters out to Cole; Cole pursues him, gun drawn, through a security checkpoint and is fatally shot by the police. As Railly holds the dying Cole, she makes eye contact with young Cole witnessing his own death, a scene to feature in Cole's countless future nightmares and leading ultimately to his selection as the scientists' 'observer'.

On the plane, Dr. Peters, safely aboard with the deadly virus, takes his place next to a woman whom we recognise as one of the lead scientists from the future. She introduces herself to him in the film's final lines: 'Jones is my name. I'm in insurance.' Outside in the parking lot, young James Cole's eyes follow the plane that will carry the virus to the next major city. Closing credits roll to the strains of Louis Armstrong's 'What a Wonderful World'.

Footnotes

1. In the 1990s, often referred to as 'The Decade of Money, Mega-Spending and Special Effects' (Dirks, 'The History of Film: The 1990s'), production costs sky-rocketed. In 1995, the year *12 Monkeys* was released, the average Hollywood budget for a feature film was $50.4 million (Eller, 'Average Cost'). A science-fiction film, often requiring both more expensive sets and more special effects, could cost considerably more. The parsimonious budgets of *Congo* and *Outbreak* (both 1995, $50 million each) still exceeded *12 Monkeys'* production costs by $20 million. Films of the mid-1990s that, like *12 Monkeys*, stage either dystopian societies or end of the world-scenarios tended to be considerably more expensive: *Mortal Kombat* (1995, $70.54 million); *Judge Dredd* (1995, $90 million), *Waterworld* (1995, $175 million), *Independence Day* (1996, $75 million), *Alien: Resurrection* (1997, $75 million) and *Volcano* (1997, $90 million) all blew *12 Monkeys'* $30 million budget out of the water.

2. The statistics and the Gilliam quotation are taken from Marks, *Terry Gilliam*, the citation p. 152. For basic information about location and casting, see also Bob McCabe, *Dark Knights*, pp. 161-70, and the interviews with Gilliam assembled by Sterritt and Rhodes. On the film's

cinematography, see Pizzello.

3. Emanuel Levy, 'Review of *12 Monkeys*', 12 August 2005 (https://www.rottentomatoes.com/m/12_monkeys/).

4. Channel 4 Film Review, *Rotten Tomatoes*, 27 May 2011 (https://www.rottentomatoes.com/m/12_monkeys/).

5. Fried, '12 Monkeys', p. 48.

6. Bob Stinson, 'Critic Reviews for *Twelve Monkeys* (*12 Monkeys*)', *Rotten Tomatoes*.

7. See, for instance, Canavan (Foucault), Cridland (Nietzsche, Heidegger, Deleuze), Del Rio (Heidegger and Foucault), Faunce (Freud), Fry and Craig (Bakhtin), and Lashmet (Foucault).

8. Greenberg, '12 Monkeys', p. 126.

9. My synopsis is based on my own repeat viewings of the film, but I have also checked my version of events against both Wikipedia and IMDb—not because I consider them the most reliable sources, but because they are most likely the first go-to sites for people seeking basic information. See plot synopses of *12 Monkeys* at Wikipedia (https://en.wikipedia.org/wiki/12_Monkeys#Plot) and IMDb (https://www.imdb.com/title/tt0114746/plotsummary).

2. Pushing the (Reset) Button: Why You Can't Start Over

12 Monkeys was an unqualified commercial success, but it remains Gilliam's least understood film, both on and beyond the plot level. Aside from recognisable debts to specific films such as *La Jetée* (1962, dir. Chris Marker) and *Dr. Strangelove* (1964, dir. Stanley Kubrick), the film plays with a number of genres (apocalypse and post-apocalypse movies; sci-fi; nuclear noir, and what is becoming known as 'geek dystopia') and themes (time travel; free will v. determinism; mental illness; conspiracy theories; the impossibility of human closeness, and the nature of reality). Intertextual links identified in literature on the film range from Frank Baum's *The Magic of Oz* to Omar Khayyám and *The Rubáiyat*, the *Book of Revelations*, Virgil's *Aeneid*, Hesiod, and Mary Shelley's *Frankenstein*, in addition to *La Jetée*, the Marx Brothers' *Monkey Business* (1931, dir. Norman McLeod), Hitchcock's *Vertigo* and *The Birds* (1963), and a variety of songs, academic lectures and psychiatric theories.[10] Nearly 25 years after the film's appearance, as movie blogs without number document, it is still a mystery to many. One reason is that *12 Monkeys* deliberately confounds viewer expectations raised by its referencing of genres and themes.

This applies particularly to the two cinematic genres that seem to offer the most obviously appropriate context for Gilliam's work: post-apocalypse films and time-travel movies. *12 Monkeys* pokes sinister fun at the contemporary tradition of post-apocalypse movies, which are profoundly indebted to the illusion that no matter how great the devastation, it is always possible to start over. Barring external reasons for Armageddon such as asteroids or alien invasion, such movies, many released around the same time as Gilliam's film, tend to trade simultaneously on human failings (some incompetent or evil bastard has pushed the button and destroyed the world) and the so-called indomitable human spirit, encapsulated in an upbeat ending in which the death of billions barely rates a mention. Post-apocalypse, the films' focus shifts immediately and optimistically to the handful of survivors who have presumably profited from these deaths as an object lesson. Having reformed, repented and survived, they lead the considerably reduced but now more robust human race into the next era. Miraculously, starting over even holds out the promise of a harmonious equality in the new world that was firmly out of reach in the old. We might think here of the rousing speech offered by the US president at the end of *Independence Day* (1996, dir. Roland Emmerich), who predicts that from the ashes of the world, a new, united humanity will arise: 'We can't be consumed by our petty differences anymore. We will be united in our common interests.' Likewise, at the end of *Volcano* (1997, dir. Mick Jackson), the near-total destruction of L.A. by a volcano is alleviated considerably by a little boy who, in the film's final scene, points at white and black survivors covered in volcano ash and exclaims: 'Look at their faces. They all look the same!'

12 Monkeys holds out no such hope that post-apocalyptic humanity will be able simply to push the reset-button, either in terms of sheer survival or in terms of social harmony. The future it portrays is a dark and sinister place where the few survivors of the apocalypse live miserably in underground cages, imprisoned for crimes that no just society would recognise, and in thrall to scientists who use them as lab rats for time-travel experiments. Whatever Armageddon has done to its survivors, it has not made them stronger, happier or fairer.

Time travel, the sci-fi genre's infallible cure-all, comes in for a similar drubbing in *12 Monkeys*, although this aspect of Gilliam's film is even less understood than its relentless undercurrent of hopelessness. Particularly scholars who have compared *12 Monkeys*—usually unfavourably—with its precursor *La Jetée*[11] tend to impose on Gilliam's film either a simplistic narrative structure or an optimism-through-the-backdoor that simply isn't there. In *La Jetée*, a time traveller falls in love with a woman of the past, rejects his present (her future) and attempts to live in the past permanently. He is shot dead by a policeman from the future, fulfilling the traveller's premonition (or memory) from the opening scene, in which a child (who will become the time traveller) witnesses a man's death (his own). Comparers of both films tend to note that both *La Jetée* and *12 Monkeys* employ a circular rather than linear narrative structure, but they seem nevertheless incapable of reading *12 Monkeys* in any way other than the linear, in other words: with an eye to the 'future'. Del Rio's comment that *12 Monkeys* 'seems to imply that the overseeing community of "good" scientists from the future will ensure that the virus is kept at bay',[12] or Canavan's statement that the goal of time travel is 'to investigate and perhaps prevent the release of an artificially created virus that will soon kill billions'[13] represent a fundamental misunderstanding of the film's final scene, even a misinterpretation of the film's most basic ideas about time. In *12 Monkeys*, the viral plague that has wiped out the world has already occurred, and numerous statements throughout the film confirm that time travel can neither prevent it nor contain it.

12 Monkeys breaks with the optimistic tradition of *both* post-apocalypse movies (the illusion that it is always possible to start over) *and* that of sci-fi movies (in which the purpose of time-travel is often to prevent a past disaster before it occurs). The reason is centrally bound up in the film's ideas about the nature of reality, which differs radically from that advanced in most other apocalypse or time-travel movies. If there is any statement that *12 Monkeys* has to make about either time travel or the End of the World, it is simply this: You can't start over. You can't change a reality that has already occurred. *You* may be able to go back in time, but you can't turn *it* back.

Footnotes

10. List and discussion in Marks, *Terry Gilliam*, p. 161.
11. Among them Del Rio in 'The Remaking of *La Jetée*' and Rafferty in 'Time Out Of Joint.'
12. Del Rio, 'The Remaking', p. 384.
13. Canavan, '"You can't change anything"', p. 92.

3. 'Thank you, Einstein': Why You Can't Turn Back Time

Terry Gilliam's drawing for the opening credits (figure 2), showing monkeys following each other in a never-ending spiral,[14] already contains the film's heftiest hint at the one point without which it cannot be properly understood: that *12 Monkeys* does not present time as linear. While we tend to associate non-linear time with time travel and futuristic scenarios, it is worth reminding ourselves that the idea has been around for centuries. The Aztec calendar, for example (figure 3), to which Gilliam's drawing bears some resemblance, relied on an interconnected tripartite system that assigned each day a unique combination of a name, number, symbol and patron deity (in this system, '12 Monkey' would have signified a date).

Figures 2 and 3: Terry Gilliam's drawing for the opening credits of 12 Monkeys *(L); Aztec calendar diagram (R; Wikimedia Commons)*

'In the modern world, time is often imagined as a straight line running from a distant past to an infinite future but not so for the Aztecs', claims the history writer Mark Cartwright,[15] and cites the historian R. F. Townsend:

> Time for the Aztecs was full of energy and motion, the harbinger of change, and always charged with a potent sense of miraculous happening. The cosmogenic myths reveal a preoccupation with the process of creation, destruction and recreation, and the calendrical system reflected these notions about the character of time.[16]

We hardly need to infer anything as direct as an Aztec 'influence' to argue that an understanding of time as full of energy and motion, as a harbinger of change, as preoccupied with creation, destruction, and recreation, and certainly as non-linear is one of the building blocks of Gilliam's film. It is the one that can best help us decipher its otherwise mysterious statements, twists, turns and plotholes. It is also hotly debated in *12 Monkeys* blogs, where linear time at times becomes the acid test for the entire film. 'It's important to remember that time is linear, and nothing can change that. When many things take place seemingly at once, it's always linear in the end. 1990 is still before 1996', claims one blogger, who then goes on to insist that 'The truth of the matter is that James' [Cole's] life was more linear than what one might think', that 'Even though there is time-travel involved, his life was still linear', and that 'In conclusion, James Cole's life was linear.'[17]

Fervent repetitions notwithstanding, *12 Monkeys* does not actually espouse the reality of linear time, but rather a non-Euclidean understanding of spacetime.[18] We owe the knowledge that time is not actually linear—in other words, that there is no such thing as past, present or future, as we understand the terms—to Albert Einstein. Before Einstein changed our understanding of time and space (first in 1905, in his *Theory of Special Relativity*,[19] then again in 1916, in his *Theory of General Relativity*), he began by dismantling our common sense, which, while enabling us to make sense of the world, is so often just plain wrong. 'Common sense', wrote Einstein, 'consists of those layers of prejudice laid down in the mind before the age of eighteen.'[20] Common sense would insist, for example, that time passes equally quickly for everyone, and that two events occur either simultaneously or one before the other. And common sense would be mistaken. Time does not pass at the same pace for the astronaut in her capsule and the controller on the ground: it passes more slowly in the capsule. 'The astronaut has her time; the controller has his. They are not the same.'[21] But because the same laws affect the passage of time for all things inside the capsule (the astronaut's pulse, her wristwatch, the time it takes for a pot to boil), the astronaut cannot know that her time has slowed down compared to the controller's.

This immediately raises the question of *time perception*, which is not to be confused with reality. Albert Einstein, in a 'thought experiment' he developed at age 16 (and on which he later based his Theory of Special Relativity) used the term 'observers', a term constantly, and probably not coincidentally, applied to Cole in Gilliam's film. Einstein's Thought Experiment imagines two scenarios: an observer chasing an object travelling at the speed of light at the same speed would perceive it to be standing still, whereas an observer standing still would perceive it to be moving. Einstein concluded that there is no way to determine which perception is correct; depending on perspective, both realities are equally valid. Reality, in other words, cannot be measured in a beyond-perspective manner by means of referring either to space or time.[22]

If time does not pass at the same pace for everyone *and* if the perception of time is relative (in the sense that two observers will disagree on the timing of any event, and both perceptions being equally valid, neither can claim to correspond to reality), this raises the question whether two observers might also disagree on temporal *sequencing*. Could a situation arise where one of two observers watching a boy throw a stone and break a window sees the window break *before* the stone is thrown? Einstein's answer is no. The order of causally linked events is never in doubt: effect always follows cause. Einstein concludes from this that causality is the only objective reality, because while observers will always disagree on the time elapsed between two events and the space between them, they will also always agree on their sequence. Time, in other words, is not responsible for causality, but the other way around.

Einstein's mathematics professor Hermann Minkowski said that the way common sense insists we think about time (as a one-dimensional timeline, leading from past to present to future) and space (a three-dimensional space that is *separate* from time) is fundamentally flawed, as is the way in which we measure space (for example, with a ruler) or time (for example, with a clock). All of these measurements are appearances, not the real thing; and all will change depending on the observer's viewpoint. Human perceptions of space and time, Minkowski claimed, are not objectively real because they don't correspond to anything per se; they are merely an imposition the human brain makes in order to make sense of the world. Rather than thinking of three-dimensional space and—separately—of a one-dimensional timeline, we should be thinking of a four-dimensional reality that includes *both* space and time and that he called 'spacetime'. Its content is neither spatial nor time measurements but *events*. All observers, Minkowski claims, will disagree about the time that has passed and the distance travelled; but all will agree about the causal relationship between events. The fact that there is universal agreement on this strengthens the case for spacetime being objective reality.

In four-dimensional spacetime, nothing ever changes. All of time, which is not separate from space but merely one of spacetime's four axes, exists on an equal footing. Events that we think of as no longer existing because they are in the 'past' exist in spacetime. Events we think of as non-existent because they are in our future and we can't perceive them yet exist in spacetime. The past, in other words, 'still exists and the future also exists and is merely waiting for us to come across it'.[23] Common sense, of course, would disagree because human perception tends to privilege the present over both the past, which it can only remember, and the future, which it cannot perceive at all. 'For some unknown reason, consciousness seems to act like a searchlight scanning progressively along the time axis, momentarily singling out an instant of physical time as being that special moment we label "now"—before the beam moves on to pick out the next instance to be so labelled.'[24] But this is *perception*, not reality: in reality, all time exists on an equal footing; causal relations of events, which correspond to spacetime intervals, are the only thing that is real; and since the future, like the past and present, already exists, nothing ever changes.

There are good reasons to see *12 Monkeys* as Einstein and Minkowski would have seen it, namely in terms of events and causality, not, as common sense would tempt us to do, in terms of linear time. Doing this would certainly answer a lot of questions that have baffled critics and bloggers for decades. Why, Canavan muses, are the film's scientists merely keen to identify the original virus at the time it is released, which gives them a chance to develop a serum for the future but does nothing to prevent Armageddon in the present? 'Why not attempt to intervene at an earlier moment—stop Dr. Peters before he leaves his house that morning, or, indeed, murder him years before he gets his medical degree? The scientists have any number of potential points of intervention; they choose not to intervene at all.'[25] Such a statement clearly assumes linear time; it supposes that the future not only follows but also depends upon the past, and that therefore you can go back and 'fix it' (it also assumes they know that Peters is the culprit, which they don't). 'Of course,' Canavan continues, the scientists 'claim it is impossible—but since we never see them try, we just have to take their word for it.'[26] Not theirs, actually: Einstein's.

For an interpretation of Gilliam's film that answers these and innumerable other questions, we should assume two basic premises—our take-away from Einstein's and Minkowski's ideas about time:

1. In four-dimensional spacetime, there is no such thing as linear time. The past does not precede the present, just as the future does not follow after the present. These are merely perceptions (illusions) that help humans interpret the world. And these are also the perceptions (illusions) that *12 Monkeys* plays with. They are the film's elaborate red herrings. In physical reality (and in the film's reality as well), all timelines exist 'simultaneously' (although that word has no meaning in four-dimensional spacetime: where there is no Before or After, there can also be no simultaneity).

2. In four-dimensional spacetime, *nothing ever changes*. For our reading of the film, this also means that Cole can't change anything. The purpose of time travel, in other words, is not to change the future (which is impossible in any event, since the future already exists).

Based on these two propositions, I would argue that *12 Monkeys*, far from being an incomprehensible mess,[27] understands its own assumptions about time rather well. The first thing it does, as did Einstein at the outset of his *Special Relativity*, is to dismantle the supremacy of common sense. Knowledge and understanding in *12 Monkeys* are the exclusive province of those bereft of common sense, the film's fruitcakes and nutjobs who people the city's lunatic asylums and street corners, from where they screech their knowledge of the End of Days at hapless passers-by. Likewise, Cole's knowledge of imminent apocalypse and his talk of different timelines is incomprehensible to the 'sane' (that is, people unable to perceive anything but the present in linear time), leading inevitably to a diagnosis of insanity followed by internment. Yet Cole is not the only 'insane' person who understands, far better than the sane ever could, that neither time nor space are what they seem. Consider, for example, Jeffrey Goines, who tells Cole that if he wants to watch a specific TV programme, he must tell the nurse before the show airs, and then launches into a rant about a patient who always requests shows after they've already played. 'No!', Goines raves, 'You have to tell her *before*! He couldn't quite grasp the idea that the charge nurse couldn't make it be yesterday. She couldn't turn back time, thank you, Einstein! Now he, he was nuts! He was a fruitcake, Jim!' It is one of the many cryptic winks the film drops its viewers: a situation is related that only makes sense if we assume that linear time is real, simultaneously referring us to the scientist who is responsible for showing us that it's not. Just as Cole's knowledge of the world's imminent end is ordinary in one timeline and aberrant in another, Goines' quotation of Einstein is simultaneously nonsensical and correct: if, as Einstein claimed, linear time is an illusion, there is neither a Forward nor a Back to which time could be turned.

Cole himself repeatedly insists that he has not returned to the past to change the future, that his role is merely to gather information which 'Won't help you. Won't help anyone. Won't change anything.' The future already exists and cannot be changed. Asked why he has come back, he offers the answer fed him by the scientists: 'Cos I'm a good observer' (by implication someone who does not intervene in events). Cole's role as a mere observer, rather than saviour of the human race, is established in the very first scene showing young Cole observing his own death—a close-up of young Cole's eyes over the sound of a gunshot. Thus the film implies from the outset that time is not linear, for the beginning is also the end. And yet there is no way of determining whether the reason for Cole's selection is a vision (presumably of the 'future') or a memory (presumably of the 'past'). Believers in linear time would have to conclude that if Cole has a vision, it is only because he's been there before (a case of 'là j'étais'). But as soon as we think of time not as a straight line leading from past to present to future but as circular (like Gilliam's drawing of the endless circle of monkeys), or bending in- and outward (like Minkowski's vision of a saddle-shaped four-dimensional spacetime), there is no longer any way to resolve the chicken-and-egg question, no way to determine what is memory and what is anticipated future.

A conversation with Railly reveals that we would be well advised to read Cole's, or indeed anyone's, observer-role in Einstein's sense, as a mere marker of 'position' that does not correspond to any reality whatsoever:

Cole. This is October, right?

Railly. April.

Cole. What year is this?

Railly. What year do you think it is?

Cole. 1996.

Railly. That's the future, James. Do you think you're living in the future?

Cole. 1996 is the past.

Railly. No, 1996 is the future. This is 1990.

This appears to be a debate about something completely beside the point, and rightly so, since the conversation focuses on time and time is beside the point. What we have here is a truly Einsteinian situation. Two observers observe time from their perspective, and both are absolutely correct from their point of view. One observer is himself moving in time and thus perceives the object of pursuit—in this case the year 1996—to be standing still (both 1990 and 1996, from Cole's perspective, are in the past). The other observer, herself fixed in a permanent present, perceives the object of pursuit to be moving, i.e. stretching into the 'future' (from her perspective, 1996 follows 1990). Neither perspective, however, corresponds to reality, simply because the discussion is about something that *has* no relation to reality—time, not events. As soon as Cole moves on to what actually constitutes reality—namely events—he is steered back to that which doesn't matter, namely time:

Cole. Five billion people died in 1996 and 1997. Almost the entire population of the world. Only about one per cent of us survived.

1990s Psychiatrist. Are you going to save us, Mr. Cole?

Cole. How can I save you? This already happened. I can't save you. Nobody can. I am simply trying to gather information to help the people in the present trace the path of the virus.

1990s Psychiatrist. We're not in the present *now*, Mr. Cole?

Cole. No. 1990 is in the past. This already happened.

All conversations reaching across timelines are 'relative' in the sense that all statements made by both observers of reality are true from their perspective but also fundamentally incompatible, which means that neither has more than a nodding acquaintance with objective 'reality'. The attendant who first describes Cole to Railly as 'totally disoriented, doesn't know where he is, what day of the week it is, all that stuff' is quite right from his present-day viewpoint: Cole, having missed the arrival target by six years, does not have the slightest idea where, or when, he is; he has no way of determining what year it is, never mind the day of the week. The conclusion the attendant draws from all this, however—that Cole is crazy—is untrue, at least from the perspective of the future. Conversely, Cole's statement that air in the 1990s is 'very fresh. No germs,' while perfectly sensible for someone coming from a germ-diseased future, sounds exceedingly odd to Railly. Most of the disconnect in the early exchanges between Cole and Railly is caused by the simple fact that while he is telling it to her straight, she is merely humouring (and attempting to diagnose) a madman. Statements that make perfect sense in Cole's timeline are irrational in Railly's. Time, or rather, the observer's perceived position in time is, in fact, the *only* difference between the observer's understanding of madness or sanity. Or, to put it slightly differently: the factor that will foil any observer's ability to interpret reality, every time, is time.

12 Monkeys turns out to be less about time-travel or even about time itself (in the sense of a dystopian 'future' caused by catastrophic events in the 'present') than about the human *perception* of time. The problem the film identifies is the general human inability to perceive anything beyond the present moment. To the human mind, the future is non-existent and the past opaque. Nothing shows this more clearly than the scene in which Cole confronts Jeffrey Goines at the gala dinner. Cole, believing Goines to be the author of Armageddon, tells him that he is not there to prevent the release of the virus: 'I can't do anything about what you're going to do. I can't change anything. I won't stop you—I just want the information.' In response, Goines accuses Cole of having planted the idea for a killer virus during their meeting in the mental hospital in 1990. He recalls Cole as having been

> all upset about the desecration of the planet, which I understand, but then you said to me, Wouldn't it be great if there was a germ, or a virus that'd wipe out all of mankind? [...] And I told you my father was this famous virologist, and you said, Hey, he could make the germ and we could steal it.

None of this bears any relation to the conversation as shown on screen earlier. That Goines misremembers the exchange to such a degree is useful in establishing that he is not, in fact, the originator of the virus. More importantly, though, it also shows that 'observing' the past is a highly inaccurate science. Cole, too, does not remember the exchange—understandably, since he was fuzzy with drugs. Thus Cole can only take Goines' word that the scene occurred as he describes it, which flings Cole into paroxysms of doubt that he may have in some way been responsible for wiping out the human race. Human perception, as this scene establishes, is permanently stuck in the present moment, its knowledge of the past unreliable, its knowledge of the future non-existent.

The film's statement that perception is limited to the present is underlined by the fact that other timelines as represented in the film are nearly totally deprived of the positive emotions with which they are commonly associated. Just as the future in *12 Monkeys* does not embody hope, the past is not charged with nostalgia (only Cole is nostalgic about the past, and only at times when he either experiences it as his present or hopes to turn it into his present). In fact, nobody but Cole cares about the past. Cole's insistence that the past can't be changed carries a note of despondency, but the scientists wouldn't change it if they could, contemptuously referring to pre-apocalypse Earth as 'that dying world'. The future, while having afforded humanity some technological advances such as the capacity for time travel, is not defined by greater knowledge, wisdom or accuracy of perception. The science of the future is rife with blunders and mis-steps;[28] as the voice in Cole's head puts it, 'science ain't an exact science with these clowns'. The scientists' first attempt to transport Cole to 1996 is off by six years; their second by eighty. They take decades to decode phone messages and are phenomenally bad at reading their test subject (at a point when all Cole wants is to return to the 1990s and live there permanently, they still think they can tempt him with a pardon). They don't know how the virus originated, only where and when—from Cole's nightmares (memories) of the shooting he witnessed at that very point in time (on the same day) and space (at the same airport). For this reason and for this reason alone, the otherwise unreliable and recalcitrant Cole becomes the scientists' prime 'observer'. They are astonishingly cold-hearted, using humans as lab-rats and caring neither about the demise of millions nor Cole's, whose death in pursuit of the culprit is the clue they need to identify the originator of the virus.

One of the conceits of other time-travel films that *12 Monkeys* does away with is the idea that the future differs significantly from the present. In fact, the pre-apocalyptic present/past and the post-apocalyptic future are remarkably similar. Dystopian dreariness permeates all timelines, and visual parallels abound—between the cityscapes of the past and the apocalyptic landscape of the future, between the mental hospitals of the 1990s and the subterranean cages of the 2030s, between the CAT-scan machine used to trace the source of mental illness and the time machine used to trace the virus. In both past and future, scientists are in total control over others whom they are free to imprison as insane or anti-social. In both timelines, Cole is deloused, brutally scrub-brushed, interrogated, drugged, chained and locked up.[29] The 'apocalyptic future', as one critic has justly remarked, is 'a direct parallel of the life we live now'.[30] Although past and future are separated by the one event that supposedly changed everything—universal apocalypse—past and future stubbornly continue to behave as if nothing had changed. Once we have let go of the idea of linear time, this only makes sense, for in four-dimensional spacetime, all timelines exist on the same footing. Reality, based on events, cause and effect, is not subject to change.

The only thing subject to change is the observer's perception. Perception is thus characterised by three elementary facts. It references time and space, not events. It therefore does not correspond to any objective reality. It can perceive the past only through a haze and the future not at all. It is, in other words, limited almost entirely to the present.

Footnotes

14. As numerous observers have pointed out (Craig; Fry and Craig), Gilliam employs circles and spirals at key times throughout the film. Craig has read these moments as citations of the film most directly referenced in *12 Monkeys*, namely Hitchcock's *Vertigo*, with its winding staircase, age rings in trees, the spiral in Carlotta's hair, and the swirling effects that dramatise Scotty's vertigo ('Trapping Simians', pp. 247-8).

15. See Cartwright, 'The Aztec Calendar.'

16. Townsend, *The Aztecs*, p. 127; cited in Cartwright, 'The Aztec Calendar.'

17. The unnamed blogger has posted his or her synopsis of the film, from which all quotations are taken, at http://bucephalus.tripod.com/plot.html#teeth. Matthew Ruben is the sole interpreter of *12 Monkeys* who has proposed reading it in light of the non-linearity of time (in '*12 Monkeys*, postmodernism, and the urban'), although he does not bring Einstein into it.

18. For scientists, I'll recommend getting the news straight from the horse's mouth (see Einstein, *Relativity*). For those those intimidated by advanced physics, Stannard's *Relativity* provides a good introduction. For those who need to test the waters, the YouTube video 'Are Space and Time an Illusion?' is a good start.

19. Einstein beat John M. E. McTaggart, who advanced very similar ideas in 'The Unreality of Time' (1908), by three years. What McTaggart proposed is 'that temporality isn't a feature of the universe *at all*: no event, nor any relation between events, whether played out over an instant or over centuries, has *anything* temporal about it. If time is anything at all, it is merely an effect of the mind, a subjective quirk rather than an objective fact.' On McTaggart's work, see Stagoll, 'Killing Time', the citation p. 28.

20. Cited in Stannard, *Relativity*, n. p.

21. Example and discussion in Stannard, *Relativity*, p. 7.

22. In *A Brief History of Time*, Stephen Hawking has offered one of the most concise illustrations of our understanding of space and time before and after Einstein: Einstein forced us to stop thinking of space and time as rooted in any 'reality' beyond the observer's perspective. 'Before 1915, space and time were thought of as a fixed arena in which events took place, but which was not affected by what happened in it. [...] Bodies moved, forces attracted and repelled, but time and space simply continued, unaffected. It was natural to think that space and time went on forever. / The situation, however, is quite different in the general theory of relativity. Space and time are now dynamic quantities: when a body moves, or a force acts, it affects the curvature of space and time—and in turn the structure of space-time affects the way in which bodies move and forces act. Space and time not only affect but also are affected by everything that happens in the universe' (p. 39).

23. Stannard, *Relativity*, p. 30.

24. Stannard, *Relativity*, p. 32.

25. Canavan, '"You can't change anything"', p. 100.

26. Canavan, '"You can't change anything"', p. 102.

27. See, for example, Craig's critique of Gilliam's presentation of time travel, which gets the details right but comes to the wrong conclusion: 'Gilliam is perversely obtuse about his universe's time-travel catechism. We quickly understand that the future's scientific community does not have the technology under control, for Cole is forced to survive several

glitches before he lands in 1996, his target year. The director also leaves hanging any attempt at explaining how both a young Cole and his adult manifestation can exist at the same time during the airport scene that forms the film's conclusion. Evidently Gilliam feels viewers are to await some temporal-spatial mumbo jumbo from the Time Lords of Gallifrey as justification. / The scientists' reliance on errant technology (which is often a theme of Gilliam's work) helps emphasize the overall ineptitude of those who are theoretically in charge of things' ('Trapping Simians', p. 245).

28. Noted by Canavan, '"You can't change anything"', p. 98 and 100, and Craig, 'Trapping Simians', p. 245.

29. The similarities of timelines have been noted, among others, in Canavan, '"You can't change anything"', p. 95; Del Rio, 'The Remaking', p. 392; Fry and Craig, 'A Carnival', p. 7; Rosen, *Apocalyptic Transformation*, p. 87.

30. Faunce, 'Paranoia', p. 456.

4. On Mis/Perceptions of Reality

Arts and Sciences

For a film whose most central premise is heavily indebted to science, *12 Monkeys* goes to astonishing lengths to denounce it, or, rather, humanity's unwavering belief that science and technology will cure all ills. Both technology and science are persistently discredited in the film. The scientists' time travel mechanism is, at best, a crude instrument that twice hurls Cole into the wrong time. On the second occasion, when the scientists land him in World War I after promising to send him to 1996, the voice in Cole's head tells him laconically that he was lucky not to have ended up in ancient Egypt. Psychiatry, another science of strict distinctions, is debunked by Railly, one of the discipline's practitioners, as an inconsistent thought system with no closer link to reality than any 'religion' or 'faith'. Conversely, there are constant premonitions (if such a concept makes sense in a film that proposes the unreality of time) of Cole's story in the world of 'irreality': namely, in art, TV and pop culture.

In the 1990s-set scenes, the TV is always on, forever alluding to what will happen (has happened) in a manner that ensures that the hint, if such it is, won't be taken seriously. Monkeys appear repeatedly on TVs in various scenes, gnawing on their bars, suffering in cruel experiments, or being lowered on strings. That these abuses are perpetrated on humans in nearly equal measure is alluded to in recurring parallelisms—a hamster on a wheel as Cole's blood is taken, or Goines screaming 'We're all monkeys!' to TV images of monkeys abused in the name of science.[31] On a children's TV cartoon, Professor Grozenschiffer, clearly meant to be a stereotypical Mad Scientist, brags that 'I haff invented ze time tunnel' and ominously announces that it is 'ready for experiment'. Cut to Cole, himself both time traveller and object of experiments, sleeping uneasily, dreaming of his own death. TV commercials advertise holidays in the Florida Keys, to where Cole and Railly attempt to escape at the end. Shortly before Cole's death, a scene from Hitchcock's *Vertigo* serves up yet another misleading cue about the nature of time. Finally, Railly offers a lecture on various time travellers throughout history who have predicted the demise of the world in the 1990s, a lecture that not only alludes to Cole but actually includes him (in a slide showing him in the World War I trench).

This is one of the most intriguing paradoxes of *12 Monkeys*: that the film's fictional worlds, from mythology and art to TV cartoons and commercials, are continually presented as describing reality more accurately than science, that part of the human enterprise charged with describing reality. Before we even begin to think about grand themes like insanity and predetermination, we should pause briefly to ask ourselves what this may mean for the film's basic understanding of 'reality' versus 'perception'. The concepts humans tend to rely upon the most, science and technology, are presented as unmitigated failures. Time technology fails Cole time and again; psychiatrists and doctors imprison, sedate and restrain rather than diagnose (let alone correctly) or treat patients (let alone with any degree of dignity or any level of success, as the mental hospital scenes glaringly show). Conversely, the film's most significant reality scenes are cross-cut with snippets from either TV or radio too frequently to be overlooked. 'There's the television,' Goines' prophetic voice tells Cole: 'It's all right there. All right there.' Some of these scenes, like the Professor Grozenschiffer cartoon and the scenes of monkeys in cages, are merely allusive. In others, TV functions as a signifier for misleading statements, limited understanding and consequent misperceptions of reality—much like time in its red-herring role.

Cole, whose exposure to TV and radio ended at the age of eight, retains only vague memories of either. Flung back into the 1990s, where radios blare incessantly and the TV is never off, he has no way of distinguishing between TV programmes intending to be factual (like the news or science programmes), fiction like the movies, or manipulation and suggestion in the form of commercials. Accordingly he tends to read everything literally. On the road with Railly, he listens to the radio and is deeply disappointed when Railly informs him that a commercial is not a personal message to him. In the mental hospital, he watches scientists on TV dripping nicotine into a rabbit's eyes. His despondent comment that 'Maybe the human race deserves to be wiped out' is over-interpreted by Goines as a suggestion and pronounced a 'great idea'. Cole, for his part, over-interprets a commercial for a vacation in the Florida Keys, which awakens in him a profound but confused yearning to see the ocean. The scene in which Goines engineers Cole's escape from the ward is accompanied by the Marx Brothers' *Monkey Business* blaring on TV, providing the soundtrack to Goines' attempts to wake Cole from his drug-induced stupor and to create a diversion for his escape. 'Get it?', he pokes Cole as he hands him the key: 'Mon—*key*. Mon-*key*.' Lines from a Mastercard commercial furnish the basis for his next direct message to Cole: 'A window of opportunity is opening *now*. Now's the time for all good men to seize the moment. The moment! Now's the time for all good men to seize the day! [...] Mastercard! Visa! The key to happiness!' As the TV shows Groucho, Harpo and Chico running away, Goines tips Cole out of his chair: 'Jim! Seize the moment!' As Cole stumbles to the door and fumbles with the key, Goines can be heard urging him on with the Mastercard commercial's triumphant final lines: 'The future can be yours! Last chance! Last chance! Last chance!' As Cole passes through the gate, he is briefly accosted by another patient quoting the Florida Keys commercial line, nodding at the key in Cole's hand: 'The Keys are lovely this time of year.' Regardless of how we interpret the role of the TV in this scene—as instigator, ironic commentary, or mere soundtrack—its constant presence not only invades 'reality' but also shapes it in significant ways. Cole's desire to run away to Florida, to 'seize' his 'last chance' to see the ocean, derives from a TV ad and ultimately leads him directly to the fateful airport. That the befuddled Cole is unable to distinguish between TV-reality and the room-reality, between Goines' exhortations and those of the commercial, is not in question.

The intersection of time, TV/the movies and mis/perceptions of reality recurs when Cole and Railly watch the scene from *Vertigo* in which Kim Novak points to her life dates on the cross-section of a hewn-down Sequoia tree: 'Here I was born, and there I died. It was only a moment for you. You took no notice.' It is, of course, another reminder that time is relative, based entirely on perception (hers versus the tree's) and thus not real, and also another reminder that we are unable to understand this basic fact (James Stewart's follow-up question—'Have you been here before?'—would be impossible to ask without the presupposition of linear time). In the audience, Cole remembers: 'I think I've seen this movie before. When I was a kid, I saw it on TV.' On screen, right on cue, Stewart presses Novak for details of 'before': 'When? When were you born?' Cut to Cole in the audience, whispering: 'But I don't recognise this bit.' Then, to Railly: 'It's just like what's happening with us. Like the past. The movie never changes—it can't change—but every time you see it, it seems different because you're different. You see different things.' This is Cole's epiphany of sorts, the point when he stops taking the things he sees on screens for the literal truth. But he simultaneously also takes a step that would be beyond observers stuck in the present: he understands that what applies to Hitchcock's film also applies to time. Like the film, the past cannot change because time never changes. The only thing that changes is our observation of time, and with it, our perception of reality. Thus, time is cast in the film as the most significant determining factor for reality perception of any kind. This, as we shall see, includes the difference between normality and insanity.

Mental 'Divergence'

Time is part and parcel of the distinction between reality and insanity in *12 Monkeys* because the audience, in order to make this distinction, is forced to rely almost entirely on the perspective of a time traveller—Cole. From the perspective of his 'future', his utterances, while sounding desperate, make sense; yet from the perspective of the past timelines into which he is flung (1914, 1990, 1996), he is insane (a perspective that is also easily understandable to the viewer). The audience is thus invited from the outset to accept both perspectives—Cole is sane; Cole is insane—as 'real'. This amounts to erasing the dividing line between sanity and insanity, as Railly, his psychoanalyst, ultimately does when she describes the distinction as an arbitrary perception unmoored from reality: 'Psychiatry, it's the latest religion. We decide what's right and wrong, we decide who's crazy or not. I'm in trouble here. I'm losing my faith.' So, too, should the audience. Noticeably, most inmates in the lunatic asylum say perfectly sensible things, and Goines, who is only an animal-rights activist, seems considerably crazier than Dr. Peters, the apocalypse nut who appears perfectly even-tempered and rational but ends up destroying humanity. There is, in essence, no meaningful distinction between 'mental illness' and 'sanity'. Like time, like space, the distinction relies entirely on human perception and corresponds to no reality.

The reason the film offers for this is, once again, time. People whose perception is limited to the present—that is, everyone who is not a time traveller—are incapable of interpreting events beyond that moment. All statements, all events, all people not 'readable' from this limited vantage point are immediately categorised as insane. In the mental asylum in 1990, Cole encounters a patient interned for believing that he comes from outer space, who confesses to Cole that he actually knows perfectly well that he's just an Earthling:

> It's a condition of mental divergence. I find myself on the planet Ogo, part of an intellectual elite, preparing to subjugate the barbarian hordes on Pluto. But even though this is a totally convincing reality for me in every way, nevertheless, Ogo is actually a construct of my psyche. I am mentally divergent in that I am escaping certain unnamed realities that plague my life here. When I stop going there, I will be well.

This may make sense to an Earthling in linear time, but in four-dimensional spacetime, the inmate's confession assumes a different meaning. For what applies to the inmate's vision of the planet Ogo obviously also applies to our interpretation of linear time: it is a totally convincing reality for us in every way, but nevertheless just a construct of our psyche. And yet, while the diagnosis is the same, the same remedy will not cure both ills. For the inmate, the only way to be 'well' (which actually means no more than to be accepted as sane) is to understand that Ogo is an illusion and to stop going there. Conversely, anyone who understands that linear time is an illusion and acts on this knowledge is promptly declared a crackpot. Mystifying the viewer further—and this is paralleled in exchanges between both Cole and Railly and between Cole and Goines—this is also one of the many passages where a supposedly insane person says something that is both utterly crazy in 1990 and absolutely true in Cole's world, where an intellectual elite does indeed subjugate people it views as 'barbarian hordes'. If something can be perfectly true in one timeline and deemed irrational in another, this suggests that reason and insanity are not distinct from each other or 'real' in any sense—any more than the past, present and future are—but mere impositions of the mind that help us interpret the world. 'Are you also divergent, friend?', the patient asks Cole, chummily resting his head on Cole's shoulder. To which the answer must be: only to people stuck eternally in the present and thus unable to perceive Cole as anything but 'divergent'.

While the film puts insanity on flamboyant display, what with Jeffrey Goines bouncing off the walls and other asylum inmates drooling down their chins, it equally clearly suggests that it is never 'divergent' mentality that is at issue, but merely divergent timelines and the misperceptions of reality they impose. 'Do you know what "crazy" is? "Crazy" is "majority rules"', Goines tells Cole in the asylum, and illustrates with a story about how in the eighteenth century, no sane person would have been able to imagine germs. Then along came Semmelweis (he means the nineteenth-century Hungarian physician Dr. Ignaz Semmelweis, an early pioneer of antiseptic procedures) and he was called crazy for it. Reality and insanity, Goines' story once again demonstrates, are movable feasts: it all depends on the when. As is so often the case, the narrative is illustrative while the conclusion is wrong. 'There's no right, there's no wrong, there's only popular opinion', Goines finishes with a flourish. In fact, there is a great deal more than popular opinion: there is universal agreement on causes. Semmelweis' work is the cause for our understanding of the danger of germs, an understanding not available to those living in a pre-Semmelweisian universe. A linear-time perspective would lead us to mistake this as a question of before and after, yet it really is one of cause and effect. Time is, as ever, a red herring.

As the factor that reliably leads to flawed interpretations of reality, time plays the starring role in *12 Monkeys*. Observers in the present, unable to interpret 'deviations' from their present-day viewpoints as rooted in a different time-perspective, resort inevitably to the fall-back diagnosis of insanity. But the view of time is not much better from the vantage point of the future. Even Cole, with his beyond-the-present-moment perspective, has a very fuzzy understanding of the past, expressed, for example, by his mistaking oldies from the 1950s and 60s—Fats Domino, Louis Armstrong—as contemporary to the 1990s.[32] Time in the film is presented as simultaneously misleading and illusory *per se*, and hints at its unreality are thick on the ground.

The aspect of *12 Monkeys* that has confounded viewers the most is that—true to the principle that time never changes but the observer does—it occasionally uncouples reality perception from time. The rules that tie specific *kinds* of perception to a specific time line are broken twice in the film. If recognition is tied to a past event, there can be no explanation for the fact that Railly recognises Cole when she first meets him in 1990. On this occasion, the exchange between them (Railly: 'Have I seen you some place?' Cole: 'Not possible.') merely documents both the fact of recognition and its impossibility; then time in the film moves on as if there was nothing to see here. Yet Railly's inability to let it go ('I have the strangest feeling that I've met you before', she insists; and later, to a colleague: 'But I have the strangest feeling about him. I've seen him someplace') make the paradox hard to dismiss. It has certainly stuck in the craw of critics, who have desperately sought an explanation that would work either in linear time or, failing that, at least in the context of a sci-fi movie whose approach to time travel allows for things like time loops and the eternally fixable past. Does Railly recognise Cole from the photograph showing him in the World War I trench, the image she used in her own book on doomsday prophets?[33] Is Railly herself caught in a time loop that would enable her to recognise the child at the airport in the adult Cole, in effect 'remembering' her own future?[34]

Not only does Gilliam's film absolutely refuse to explain Railly's recognition of Cole when she meets him for the first time, it compounds the mystery by repeating it. When Cole and Railly change into their holiday disguise at the movies, they recognise each other in their respective disguises, although they're seeing each other like this for the very first time. Cole's recognition of Railly is easily explained, for Railly in her blonde wig features prominently in his recurring dream of the man shot at the airport, whom Railly caresses as he dies. But how can Railly, for whom this scene is still in the future, recognise Cole in his Bermuda shirt, hat, wig and false moustache? 'I remember you like this', she tells him (not, then, as he appears in the World War I photograph).[35] 'I felt I'd known you before. I feel I've always known you.' Railly's repeated recognition of Cole at points when she sees him—or sees him 'like this'—for the first time makes sense only if we suspend our faith in linear time. The event—meeting Cole—is real; the past-tense terms she employs for the 'when' of that event ('remember', 'before', 'always') are misperceptions of reality. The event has not changed, and neither has its timing, for time never changes. What has changed is the observer—Railly herself. Is it conceivable that Railly's observation, shaped by years of research on time travellers, her contact with Cole, and her ultimate acceptance of the reality of time travel, has gained a perspective beyond linear time? Can it be that her observer's position, usually tied to the present and therefore faulty, has been moved out of the eternal present? The time signature we impose upon Railly's observation— is it pre-membrance or post-cognition?—is beside the point. The true point is made by Cole watching *Vertigo*: 'The movie never changes [...] but every time you see it, it seems different because you're different. You see different things.'

Much of the film's treatment of reality and sanity is contained in the statement that, constrained by our present-day perspective, our perception of reality is self-fulfilling, circular, and fashioned almost entirely by our expectations. (Jeffrey Goines, with his knack for making sensible statements while acting utterly mad, has one for this predicament too: 'You dumb assholes', he tells the orderlies restraining him for unruly behaviour, 'I'm a mental patient. I'm *supposed* to act out.') Time travellers and doomsday prophets—the two groups do not merely overlap but are, in fact, identical[36]—are classed as insane because we are simultaneously unable to see past the present and unable to accept that which we can't see as real. Thus these people exist outside of the tiny circle of our expectations. Railly cites a great many of them in her 1996 lecture, including a man who appeared out of nowhere in Stonehenge in April 1362, speaking unfamiliar words in a strange accent. (At this point, Gilliam's audience is already poised to identify the stranger as a time traveller accidentally dumped in fourteenth-century Stonehenge by scientists planning to send him to the United States of the 1990s, and the strange language as present-day American English.) In Railly's relation, this man 'made dire prognostications about a pestilence which he said would wipe out humanity in approximately 600 years'. Such prophets, she declares, have regularly popped up during the most catastrophic events in human history, from natural disasters like the bubonic plague to man-made horrors like the mustard gas attacks of World War I. During that war, Railly continues, her accompanying slide showing a close-up of Cole's next-cage neighbour Jose on a stretcher, a wounded soldier offered a hysterical tale. He had lost all comprehension of French but spoke English fluently, although in an unrecognisable dialect. Railly relates that this soldier, before disappearing without a trace, claimed that he had come from the future and was looking for a pure germ that would, starting in 1996, wipe mankind from the face of the earth. Her audience's chuckles express a rush to judgement: all these people were, of course, crazy as loons, just as all the other apocalyptists from the future are classed as insane from the perspective of the present —from those in Cole's head to the doomsday prophets on street corners (all of them, as we later learn, time travellers from the future hiding in the past). Railly's interpretation, while more sympathetic, is every bit as predictable because it is the only one available to a psychologist living in linear time. The soldier, she claims, had simply substituted 'for the agony of war a self-inflicted agony we call the Cassandra Complex. Cassandra, in Greek legend, was condemned to know the future but to be disbelieved when she foretold it. Hence, the agony of foreknowledge combined with the impotence to do anything about it.' Little does she know as she offers this analysis that the Cassandra Complex is also the Cole Complex, and that it will shortly also become her own.

Much of the film's time is invested in the idea that 'divergent' reality *perceptions* routinely lead to the misdiagnosis of people—most prominently, of course, of Cole— as insane. And yet Cole's reality *denial* towards the end of the film—reality denial being, in fact, a true symptom of psychosis[37]—is granted considerably less space. It is immediately followed, and thus also drowned out, by the mayhem of his death scene at the airport. Yet this remains one of the film's great ironies: that its main hero is considered insane while he is perfectly healthy and is deemed rational at a point when he is insane, in the sense of denying a reality he knows to be true.

Cole, who at the outset of the story both is sane and perceives himself as sane, travels back into a time where reality perception is hindered by the blinders imposed by an insurmountable present, rendering all distinctions, including that between insanity and normality, unreliable. And yet, ironically, he himself accepts that distinction as generally valid, although misapplied in his case. 'This is a place for crazy people. I'm not crazy', he protests when he is interned in 1990, remarking further that 'You've got some real nuts here'. He follows this up with a statement that makes him sound like one: 'I know some things that you don't know.' Yet he cannot express his knowledge convincingly because he is unable to assess his context, unaware of the fact that in the eternal present, things like time travel, imminent apocalypse, voices in your head and an irreversible future are sure signs of mental illness. As long as he is able to interpret these events from his perspective, he remains on mission and convinced of his own sanity. What drives him crazy in the end, if we accept reality denial as a sign of psychosis, is not the siren song of majority opinion that has proclaimed him insane; what drives Cole over the edge is a mixture of guilt—the thought that he himself might have planted the idea of the apocalyptic virus in Goines' mind—and addiction to 'that dying world'. The scene in which he seriously considers himself the architect of Armageddon is also the one where he waxes lyrical about the present: 'Do you think maybe I wiped out the human race? [...] I could live right here. You got water, air, stars... You can breathe. Oh, I love this world! And I love the frogs and spiders.' Shortly thereafter, he is yanked back to the future to be debriefed, and remorse about having brought about the hellish future leads him to deny it all: 'You people don't exist. You're not real. We can't travel back in time. Whoop, whoop. Uh oh. You're not here. You can't trick me. You're in my ... mind! I am insane, and you are my insanity.' It is one of the most humorous scenes of the film, what with the scientists fussing about him, tucking him in, even serenading him with his favourite '1990s' hit, Fats Domino's 'Blueberry Hill'. But it is also one of the film's most serious scenes, for it identifies guilt as the origin of insanity, just as reality denial is its major symptom. All imaginable horrors—fear, loathing, despair, the certainty of imminent death—pale beside guilt. Armageddon itself is a bearable prospect; *causing* Armageddon is not. Before Goines convinced Cole that he himself has suggested the idea for the virus, Cole was perfectly able to accept the most awful of all thinkable realities: 'Five billion people died in 1996 and 1997. Almost the entire population of the world. Only about one per cent of us survived. [...] This already happened.' But the possibility that he himself caused this event leads him to deny it all. Which is to say that it drives him insane—for insanity is the position that claims that that which may not be cannot be.

In the future, Cole, in a further ironical twist, finds himself in the same situation that he negotiated so unsuccessfully in the past: having to convince his doctors that he is sane. He only succeeds because he has finally understood that in every timeline, sanity is seen as little more than an ability to parrot the party line. 'I just wanna do my part to get us back on top, in charge of the planet', he reassures the by now deeply suspicious scientists, sounding every bit as authentic as a three-dollar bill. But it is enough to convince them to send him back to 1996, where he tells Railly, who is now convinced of the reality of time travel and imminent doom, that he is crazy and needs her help to get better. The irony here is not merely that both Cole and Railly have now finally come around to each other's previous point of view. The greater irony is that at this point, Cole *is* in fact insane—but not in the way he thinks. He is not insane in the sense that he imagines himself to be a time traveller when time travel doesn't exist. But he is insane in the sense of denying reality and supplanting it with a wished-for alternative. In an earlier scene, in which the voice in his head accused him of this very thing—that all Cole wants is 'To see the sky. And the ocean. To be topside. To breathe the air. To be with... her'—Cole screamed his denial. Now, however, safely ensconced in the hotel room with Railly, he is ready to admit it: 'I want the future to be unknown. I want to become a whole person again. I want this to be the present. I want to stay here, in this time, with you.' And yet, as his incantatory use of the words 'I want...' indicates, Cole has not yet taken up residence in Cloud Cuckoo Land, he is merely boarding the train there. He has not yet totally extinguished the difference between wishful thinking and reality. In the very next scene, Cole demonstrates that he's got a residue of rationality left, and he does it— are we even surprised anymore?—by committing an act that looks completely loony. Remarking casually that this is where the scientists from the future insert tracking devices, he breaks out his teeth, 'Just in case I'm not crazy'.

Against all the appearances of insanity that can be rationally explained—the voices in Cole's head; his foreknowledge of apocalypse; not knowing where and when he is; his inability to distinguish between TV and reality; his self-mutilation and ravings about tracking devices in teeth—the film ultimately pits two concrete definitions of the condition. Both apply to Cole at the end of the film. The first is reality denial and the substitution of a wished-for reality (Cole's version of the Planet Ogo) for the real thing. The second is Cole's refusal to acknowledge anything beyond the present, since only putting on twentieth-century blinders to the future will enable him to live in the eternal present. In the airport bathroom, where Cole fixes his fake moustache right before going to his death, the voice in his head tells him that he won't be allowed to live permanently in the present. Cole screams like the madman he is: 'This is the present. This is not the past, this is not the future. This is right now! I'm not leaving! You got that?' But of course, the voice is absolutely correct in reminding him that 'You don't belong here': 'belonging' in the present means an actual inability to perceive anything beyond the present, whereas Cole's ability to remain is predicated on a wilful disavowal of a future that he knows already exists. The true mark of Cole's insanity is that in his own mind, he is not yet crazy *enough*. 'I'm not leaving' is simultaneously a refusal to leave and an acknowledgement that it is possible to leave the present, that there is already a future waiting for him. Insanity is indicated in Cole's fervent hope that he will eventually become insane enough to believe, as completely as twentieth-century people do, in the false reality of the eternal present.

Cole, believing that the source of the voice is in one of the toilet stalls, kicks in the door, only to encounter a terrified-looking heavyset man who looks at him as if he *were* crazy. Which is, of course, both what he is and all he ever hopes to be. For only insanity, the belief in something he knows to be untrue, allows for the possibility of human closeness: 'I want this to be the present. I want to stay here, in this time, with you.'

The Cinematography of Insanity: Angles

Gilliam's cinematography weighs in heavily on the question of insanity. Its way of declaring that insanity and normalcy are merely matters of perspective is, of course, perspective. Off-kilter camera angles alternate with straight shots, with each being assigned a timeline and its viewpoint.[38] Cinematographically at least, the film tells us precisely what we'd like to hear: Railly's world (the world of linear time; the world that won't end anytime soon) is declared sane (unless, of course, we happen to be in a lunatic asylum); Cole's world (where time travel exists and the world's expiration date is upon us) is pronounced crazy. Cole's world is filmed as being off-kilter, off-putting—just *off*. Hardly ever does it feature a straight, full-frontal, unobscured view of anyone or anything. Cole's death at the airport, with which the film opens, is shot at an angle. Faces of scientists and views of the Earth's surface are crazily tilted; inmates are filmed through the wire mesh of their cages. Wide-angle shots show screaming inmates being hoisted out of their cages in chains for 'volunteer duty'. The scene in which Cole dresses himself in his rubber suit is slanted right or left, with the tilt increasing markedly over time. We, the audience, are forced to observe the future listing either to port or starboard. One of the earliest straight shots, a full ten minutes into the film, takes us to a lecture attended by Railly, where we are treated—a visual relief at this point—to full-frontal close-ups on the speaker followed by a perfectly normal-looking slow pan across the audience. But as soon as Railly leaves this bastion of learning and erudition—she is called to the holding cell to interview Cole— we are, cinematographically speaking, back in the future. The camera accompanies her on her walk past the prison cells at knee-height, lowering us, so to speak, to the prisoners' level and showing us their faces through bars and grilles.

Alternating straight and angled shots establish a pattern of destabilisation that achieves more than putting varying perspectives on insanity or normality on cinematographic display. It also indicates which perspective immediately recommends itself to the viewer as easiest to believe, and which would take a veritable leap of faith to adopt. Pushing the viewer into the perspective with which they are already the most comfortable is the job of 'normal' camera angles, and of course it is the very insistence with which these angles recommend viewpoints to us that we've always held that should make us suspicious. Camera angles tell us what is 'normal' and what is 'crazy' before we even have a chance to listen to the dialogue. Mad diagonal perspectives dominate mental institute scenes and are only interrupted by occasional angles that epitomise supervision and control (such as the slow circular panning shot showing Cole's interrogation by the group of doctors in the 1990s, an obvious parallel to his briefing by the scientists of the future in a previous scene). Off-kilter camera angles track Goines as he introduces Cole to the asylum's rules; they close in on the resident of Planet Ogo as he rests his head on Cole's shoulder; they pursue Cole as he escapes and stumbles into the MRI room at the hospital; they show him manacled to a bed after he is recaptured; they dominate the entire World War I sequence. From there, sweet relief, we are transported into the perfectly straight-perspective world of Railly's own lecture, where the camera shows us exactly what we expect to see: full frontal close-ups of her face, shot slightly from below to allow us a view of the stunning slides behind her, alternated with slow panning counter-shots of her audience. Wide-angle shots of the lecture hall reveal ornate ceilings, elegant columns, evenly spaced chairs, a large screen and tall, handsome windows. Everything breathes order and symmetry. Relax, the camera tells us: you are now in a safe space. Specifically, the camera re-enacts the absolute position of safety from which we (and Railly's diegetic audience) listen to her lecture. We are, in other words, encouraged not to take the messages of the doomsday prophets she cites seriously, just as her audience greets the news of their own imminent destruction with chuckles.

Straight-on camera angles and the temporary relief they offer are highly persuasive ways of creating a false sense of safety. They are Gilliam's way of transporting us back to known territory, only to yank us out of it again. Car scenes with Railly driving, weeping in fear of her abductor, and telling Cole he is insane are shot straight-on, from either the hood or windshield. This, the camera seems to tell the viewer, is something you should be able to handle; it's familiar territory from every crime drama and every cop flick (also, for that matter, from many Hitchcock films). Conversely, shots of Cole looking for the Army of the Twelve Monkeys at the hideout of the homeless are disturbingly slanted. Scenes in Goines' mansion showing Leland Goines' speech and Jeffrey being called away to meet Cole are slow pan shots giving a good view of the luxurious room or straight-on shots of faces. As soon as Cole enters the equation, we are back in the Land of Off-Kilter: frog or bird's-eye perspectives dominate his conversation with Goines, which mostly takes place as they walk up a large circular staircase. Crazily tilted angles accompany Goines misremembering their conversation in the asylum and his following furious rant, with the slats of the banister throwing large shadows that resemble prison bars on the wall behind them. When Goines has Cole thrown out, slanted camera angles are interspersed with circular shots panning around the spiral staircase. Tilted bird's-eye and frog-perspective shots alternate in quick succession, showing Cole on his way down the stairs, first walking, then falling, then jumping, and finally scrambling over the dining room tables. The scientists debriefing Cole on his high-up chair are shot from the frog-perspective, as are Railly and Cole entering the airport. The film ends with an extreme bird's-eye shot of young Cole and his parents getting in the car, followed by a lingering close-up of his eyes as we hear the sound of a plane taking off. When we are inside Cole's world or seeing it from Cole's perspective, we are virtually never on the level.

Throughout the film, camera angles, both straight and slanted, force the audience to question its own perspective. Extreme angles dominate many scenes featuring

Cole, scenes set in the future, mental institute scenes, and the airport death scene; and these are, literally as well as figuratively, the film's most off-putting moments, the ones that skew things, turn things on their head, tell us that reality is out of whack. Straight angles, conversely, are assigned to the normality-perception of the 1990s: Railly being abducted in her car; Railly giving or attending lectures; Railly discussing the value of her discipline with a colleague. Camera angles offer the audience a choice of perspective. As Gilliam put it, 'We live in a world, the one we dream and one that is. [...] You just have to decide which one you want to spend more time with.'[39] His camera angles not only illustrate that choice, but also imply a snarky comment on what that decision is likely to be. Even Cole, in the end, turns into a reality-denier. Few of us will choose the world 'that is' if this means accepting that Chicken Little and Cassandra were right all along. Nothing can protect us from a future apocalypse that already exists and is merely waiting for us to experience it. Most of us will be far happier to spend more time in the world we dream, even knowing it to be illusory. For this is the world that offers the comfort and familiarity of straight lines—as straight as the line leading from the past to the present to a future without end.

Footnotes

31. As pointed out, among others, in Marks, *Terry Gilliam*, p. 167.
32. Pointed out by many, for example in Marks, *Terry Gilliam*, p. 159.
33. Doubted by Fry and Craig, 'A Carnival of Apes', p. 10.
34. Suggested by Ashbrook, *The Pocket Essential Terry Gilliam*, p. 73. The time-loop theory is also entertained in Fry and Craig, 'A Carnival of Apes', p. 11.
35. Pointed out by Fry and Craig, 'A Carnival of Apes', p. 11.
36. See Rosen, *Apocalyptic Transformation*, p. 89: 'From the very beginning [...], time travel is associated with apocalyptists.'
37. See the essays assembled by Ogden and Biebers in *Psychology of Denial*.
38. On camera angles in the film, see Richardson, 'Twelve Monkeys.'
39. Gilliam cited in Rosen, *Apocalyptic Transformation*, p. 92.

5. The Human Condom and Other Signs of Loneliness

Human interaction in *12 Monkeys* suggests that closeness is virtually impossible. Whether in the 'future' or in the 'past', people are isolated from each other, imprisoned in jails or mental hospitals. The constant need to guard against infection forces future humanity into protective shells, 'human condoms'—the term is Gilliam's[40]—like Cole's latex body-armour and the space-suit-looking ensemble that shields him from infection on the surface. Nakedness is ubiquitous (Cole spends a significant amount of his screen-time unclothed), but where it appears it denotes vulnerability, not intimacy. The human body is fragmented in various ways. Teeth are used as tracking devices, then extracted. Conversations in the future don't take place face to face but with the help of a video ball that separates one person from the other and further fragments their bodies, showing only flattened faces, eyes and mouths (Figure 4).

Figure 4: Distance and fragmentation achieved through technology

Such physical isolation and fragmentation begs the same question as the film's many mythical characters, cross-over characters, look-alikes, half-remembered faces, misremembered faces and disembodied voices. Among these are Railly's repeated statements that she 'remembers' Cole (although this is impossible if we accept the reality of linear time); the disembodied voice who contacts Cole in various timelines; or the apocalypse street preacher who recognises Cole as 'one of us'. The questions the film asks constantly and never answers are: How do people know each other? Where do they know each other? *When* do they know each other? What possibilities for human closeness exist (the only examples we are offered are Cole and Railly's never-consummated love story, and ten-year-old Cole being dragged away from his adult corpse by unseen parents)? And why does communication, even about rather important things like the end of the world, so often end in total misunderstanding, as it does in the scene in which Cole and Goines remember their conversation in the mental hospital in incompatibly different ways?

Identity

Unsurprisingly for a film in which insanity takes centre stage, identity is presented as uncertain, unsettled and conflicted. Identity is utilitarian, not personal, and accordingly established via markers, not names.[41] Cole is Cole, James (his next-cage neighbour Jose actually thinks his name is Colejames), inmate number 87645. He responds to the neutral and distancing 'Mr. Cole' or the subordinating 'Cole' in both timelines, but has difficulty recognising himself when addressed less formally. Railly's attempt to personalise her first interview with him by calling him by his first name merely puzzles him: 'James', he muses. 'Nobody ever calls me that.' Other names he is called, like Jim or Jimbo (by Jeffrey Goines and an attendant at the mental hospital), friend (by the mentally 'divergent' resident of the planet Ogo), Jack (by a sleazy hotel receptionist), Bob or Bobby (by the raspy voice in his head) don't elicit a response of any kind from him. Names in Cole's future are impersonal not only in the sense that personal names are hardly ever used (the scientists only call Cole 'James' when they try to cajole him or calm him down) but also in the sense that they have been stripped of meaning beyond the simple identification of an object. They do not denote personality but merely illustrate the depersonalisation of humans. In this context, any act of naming that still indicates a person becomes significant, noble, notable. It begins to stand for meanings that, implied in the act of naming, need not be declared or enacted. How, for example, are we given to understand that Cole and Railly are in love, given the total absence of sex scenes, declarations of love, or lingering kisses accompanied by soft violin music? He calls her 'Kathryn' and she calls him 'James'. In a world in which names have lost their ability to designate the recognition of another person, much less a bond between the person naming and the person named, that is all the hint we need.

Identity in the future is formed by paradoxical simultaneities. Total separation coexists with total supervision. Everyone is lonely, yet nobody is ever alone. Inmates are kept in small cages and in full view of each other, a system that simultaneously enforces total separation and a complete lack of privacy. Beyond the observation of his own death at the airport and the recurring nightmares that result, Cole doesn't have a personal story that we know of. Yet everything about him is known, encoded in a bar-code tattooed on his neck and downloadable at any time by anyone with the right bar-code reader. Paradoxical simultaneities inform even the extra-diegetic level. As Ashbrook has cleverly remarked, the abjectly submissive James Cole bears one similarity to John McClane, the tough, rebellious cop of the *Die Hard* movies that propelled Bruce Willis to superstardom, namely 'the amount of leaking he does'. Just as McClane is forever covered in blood, most of Cole's screen time shows him sweating, weeping, drooling or bleeding: 'He just can't keep those nasty, horrible, disease-carrying bodily fluids in.'[42]

These ever-present fluids are a constant reminder of the virus, the need to find it, the need to contain it, and these mandates ultimately result in the detachment of signifiers from their original meanings, just as happens with names and identities. Nakedness, for instance, designates just about anything *except* intimacy: helplessness, physical discomfort, exposure in all senses of the word, danger, weakness and vulnerability. When Cole is sent to the germ-ridden surface, he is stripped naked, then encased in his 'human condom' of rubber and latex (Figure 5).

Visuals of leaks, like water running down the walls, and aural warnings of leaks accompany the elaborate process of putting it on. 'All openings of your garment must be sealed completely', a loudspeaker blares. 'If the integrity of the suit is compromised in any way, if the fabric is torn or a zipper not closed, readmittance will be denied.' Cole in his full-body condom, looking simultaneously naked and like a spaceman, enters a tube, is disinfected with a poisonous-looking green-yellowish gas, and rides up an elevator to a dark, wet, industrial landscape where water pools and drips and waterfalls gush from ceilings. Returned from the surface, he is disinfected again and scraped brutally by men encased in plastic body armour, then draws his own blood to more threats emanating from the loudspeaker: 'If there are any indications of contamination by germs, the subject will be denied entry into the

Figure 5: Colejames (Bruce Willis) encased in plastic, on his way to the contaminated surface of the Earth

secure population.' Just as in the scene in which Cole is interrogated by the scientists, manacled to a chair that could stunt-double for an electric chair and hoisted half-way up a wall (Gilliam: 'It's like a butterfly stuck on a wall, pinned down by scientists observing and dissecting it')[43], paradoxical simultaneities abound: Cole is simultaneously allowed inside and kept at a distance. He is constantly leaking fluids and forever being 'cleansed'—deloused, disinfected, scrubbed, jet-sprayed, his head shaved because 'hair is dirty'. He is both naked and clothed; both totally alone and never left alone: he is constantly recognised—by Railly, by random doomsday prophets who point and shout at him. He is forever connected to something— manacled or chained, his skin pinched by contacts, cables, and tubes—and yet also disconnected from everything and everyone (Figure 6).

Paradoxical simultaneities plague not only Cole but anyone who is not a member of the 'secure population', that is, 'normal people' and those who fancy themselves such. All prophets and doom-criers are similarly naked or incompletely covered and leaking: Jose naked and bleeding in a ditch in World War I; bums clad in rags, spittle flying as they deliver their doomsday messages; inmates in hospital pyjamas with parts of their bodies exposed, drooling down their chins. Much like Cole, all of them speak without being believed, all are kept safely away from 'the secure population', and all are possessed of a frail identity. Some members of this mad tribe, like the voice in Cole's head, remain invisible, unidentifiable. Others do their best to conceal their identity, like the bum who breaks out his teeth to remove the trackers hidden in them. And none, with the exception of Cole and Jose, are identified by name.

*Figure 6: Cole James
encased in plastic,
naked and leaking*

Communication

A fragmented, uncertain, vulnerable, paradoxical or rejected identity provides a
poor basis for communication with others since there is literally no 'I'-position from
which one could speak to another. Just as nakedness denotes not intimacy but
vulnerability, links in the film denote confinement rather than connectedness. There
are things tethering humans (cables, tubes, manacles, the chains on which screaming
'volunteers' are hoisted out of their cages), but it is not often clear to what. The
same paradigm of one-sidedness pervades almost all communication in the film.
When people talk, they talk at each other, not to each other, and often without any
expectation of a response or even of being listened to—like a doomsday messenger
on a street corner.

What starts the plot of *12 Monkeys*, keeps it going and hurls it towards its sinister
conclusion is Cole's dream of the man at the airport, born of his childhood memories
of watching him die, because these dreams (memories) are the reason the scientists
select him as their 'observer'. By definition, dreams and memories are things
experienced individually; to be released, they must be communicated. And yet, when
Cole speaks about his dreams, when Railly speaks about 'remembering' Cole, both
are half-talking to themselves. These statements are not really addressed to the other
person at all; they express more confusion than communication. Sometimes these
statements to the self are mistaken by someone else as actual communication, as
happens when Cole mutters to himself that 'Maybe the human race deserves to be

wiped out' and Goines mistakes this for an action plan. The statement is made and heard, but it is one-sided in the sense that it never arrives: speaker and listener infer different meanings and later remember the conversation in incompatible ways.

Other examples of one-sided communication include the film's many disembodied voices, from partially erased telephone messages to the voices in Cole's head. Both are garbled and largely incomprehensible, and both are unidirectional in the sense that they merely provide information or issue orders. Just as the scientists are spurred into action by the phone messages, the little voices in Cole's head tell him what to do. Both are of obscure origin: just as the scientists don't know who left the phone message about the Army of the Twelve Monkeys, Cole does not know who, if anyone, is the owner of the voice he hears, or how this voice has gained access to him. Real communication requires an opposite that can be recognised and therefore understood, and that, as the voice informs Cole, is precisely *not* the point. Who and where is the owner of that voice? He tells Cole that he is 'in another cell, maybe', and then 'clarifies': 'Maybe means, maybe I'm in the next cell. Another "volunteer", like you. Or maybe I'm in the central office, spying on you for all those science bozos. Or hey, maybe I'm not even here. *Maybe* I'm just in your head. No way to confirm anything.' The point is not to communicate but to keep Cole confused.

In both timelines, communication is understood not as the key to unravelling the mystery of the virus and therefore as potential salvation, but as profoundly unsafe. As Cole experiences several times in both his time and Railly's, making the slightest move to approach another human being physically is viewed as a threat severe enough to bring the orderlies running. Any communication of any kind must be prefaced by endless assurances that he won't hurt his interrogators, and the anxiousness with which the doctors of the past keep their distance from Cole is exaggerated to the point of absurdity in the debriefing scene in which the scientists of the future chain Cole to a chair and hoist him half-way to the ceiling (Figure 7).

The high chair and the video ball through which Cole addresses the scientists (both Gilliam's additions, not part of the Peoples's script) are another splendid example, perhaps the film's most forceful, of one-sided communication. What mattered to Gilliam was the idea that technology serves only its masters, and that the masters

Figure 7: Colejames, manacled to a chair and 'communicating' with a video ball

employ technology not to communicate but to confuse:

> ...the scientists are seeing their subject—a guy up there on the wall—in a clearly defined way; while, from his point of view, it's just chaos and confusion, and he can barely see who's there. His viewpoint is a more confused one, because his direct view of them is interfered with by the technology. So what's the statement here? That we use television and movies as mirrors that supposedly show us the world, but it's distorted; or that we communicate to each other through these things and less and less directly.[44]

Goines does Gilliam one better by defining communication not merely as a distortion but as a kind of virus, as he explains to Cole why he won't be permitted a telephone call:

> Telephone call. That's communication with the outside world. Doctor's discretion. Nuh-uh. If all of these nuts could just make phone calls, it could spread. Insanity oozing through telephone cables, oozing into the ears of all these poor sane people, infecting them. Wackos everywhere, plague of madness.

If communication is dangerous and can spread like an infection, it must be guarded against and contained. This is the role assigned to technology in the film. Almost all significant communications take place indirectly, with technology impeding and delaying understanding rather than mediating it. The most important information about the virus comes from two phone messages, both garbled and partially erased, and both directly contradictory of each other—one informs the scientists that the

Army of the Twelve Monkeys are the originators of the virus, the other tells them they're not. Technology, in other words, is a highly effective means to control people, to imprison them, coerce them, track them and spy on them. As Jeffrey Goines reminds us in his rant about scientists X-raying his brain, developing a probability matrix and predicting his every possible future thought before it even occurs to him, the possibilities are endless when it comes to evil uses of technology. Yet when it comes to beneficial uses or even simple problem-solving, technology is a near-complete failure. Time-travel targets are missed by years or decades. Simple phone messages take decades to decode. And the one positive use to which technology and science are put, developing the serum, is not intended to save the Earth or even a single life, but merely to extend the tyrannical scientists' rule from the underground to the Earth's surface.

The Cinematography of Loneliness: Spaces

Spaces in *12 Monkeys* are isolating, overwhelming, dark and confusing. Philadelphia, with its birth-of-the-nation connotations, proved a particularly apt location for an Armageddon movie because so much of it was falling apart, said Jeffrey Beecroft, the film's production designer, adding that he and Gilliam 'returned again and again to the central image of "a mouse in a maze"'.[45] Plans to shoot in England were quickly abandoned because there were 'no suitably dire underground locations and not enough abandoned buildings. '"We went to Philadelphia looking for rotting America," Gilliam told *Entertainment Weekly*. "It turned out to be the perfect place."'[46] Gilliam, whose tight budget prohibited the erection of expensive sets in any event (Beecroft's budget was a minuscule $3.5 million, for 65 shooting days on 127 different sets),[47] gamely called this 'the found-art approach':

All the decay we found in that city made it the right place to be.

The film is about a nostalgic sense of loss, a doomed civilization; and there's Philly, the former capital of the country, with two big power stations empty and redundant because all the industry moved west after the war.[48]

Philadelphia's abandoned warehouses and urban decay provide the dystopian sets of the future, most of which are inside spaces: vast floor areas strewn with trash, abandoned machinery and invaded by undergrowth; tall walls and ceilings with holes through which water gushes down and runs down walls; huge dimly lit caverns into which thousands of tiny cages are crammed to house the prisoners; large artificially lit work spaces for the scientists, stuffed chaotically with leaflets, posters, books, tables and chairs, video equipment, cables, pumps and industrial machinery. If, in the future, outside spaces are unfit for human habitation and inside spaces unbearable to live in, the 1990s shots show us a Philadelphia well on its way there, with its former grandeur only emphasising its decline. It is a dark town that shares with its future incarnation large wire mesh fences, dirty and trash-littered streets, and vapour and mist rising incongruously from the ground. Just as you will in the future, you have to watch where you step. Tall, imposing buildings with large columns are defaced by graffiti and posters. Outside, the homeless warm their hands on fires in barrels. The sleazy pay-by-the-hour hotel into which Cole and Railly check in was once a palatial building of large rooms, grand staircases, huge windows, ornate wall carvings and solid mahogany panelling. The cinema in which Cole and Railly see *Vertigo*, once a lavish space, is grubby and mostly empty, with sticky floors and stuffing spilling out of the seats. Faded glory greets the eye wherever we go: just like the Philadelphia of Cole's future, the Philadelphia of the 1990s implies a glorious past that no longer exists. Towards the end of the film, the point is made more insistently, by repeatedly superimposing Cole's future over scenes taking place in the past. Railly's freshly spray-painted message is counter-cut with the same message as Cole remembers it, faded but legible, in 2035; the hole in the department store ceiling and pigeons flying through it is superimposed briefly over the as-yet intact ceiling in the same store, where Cole and Railly buy their disguises; the department store angel, raised on ropes behind Cole as they shop, intuits not only the same angel he saw in 2035 on his cockroach-collection tour but also the 'volunteers' yanked out of their cages in chains.

Mice in a maze, a sense of loss, a doomed civilisation. The film translates these ideas into basic emotions—confusion, mourning, hopelessness and existential loneliness— and expresses these emotions spatially. It does this in five major ways: by juxtaposing faces with spaces, high with low, inside with outside, fictional spaces with real, and by *failing* to juxtapose past spaces with those of the future.

Faces in *12 Monkeys* often anticipate spaces. Our first visual encounter with Cole is a cut from an extreme close-up of young Cole's eyes to an extreme close-up of adult Cole's eyes. While this establishes his identity along a timeline—he is that boy; he will become that man—we have no way of knowing who he is because we don't know, for long seconds, *where* he is. Our first view of adult Cole shows shadows of wire mesh on his sleeping face in close-up, then another close-up of his face as he wakes up. Why does he wake up? Because there is light on his face. We have a split second to infer the obvious: this man is waking up in his bed because sunlight has hit his face. But then the light moves on. Not sunlight, then. At this point the camera pans out to reveal where we are: he is in a cage; there is another cage immediately adjacent with another person in it, and another after that and another after that and so on, as far as the eye can see. What we mistook for sunlight is the beam of a flashlight held by a guard, obviously checking that all the animals are safely in their cages. The slow-reveal sequence about Cole's location is also one about his identity: we surmise, correctly, that he was once the boy in the previous scene. We surmise, incorrectly, that he is a regular guy waking up in a regular bed. We find out, finally, that he is a convict, a criminal, or a caged animal.

Extreme close-ups of faces or body parts are one of the film's most regular features. They achieve above all two things: isolating or even fragmenting the person under the microscope and withholding his context. Cole undergoing the elaborate procedure of donning the latex suit is filmed in the same way. A close-up focuses on his hand as he puts on the gloves; another on the back of his head as he pulls on the rubber cap; a full body shot (tilted, of course) as he pulls on his latex socks are followed by alternating diagonal left and diagonal right shots as he dons the suit. He is sent up to the surface in an elevator, but there is, again, a delay of several seconds before the camera tells us this in no uncertain terms. At first we see only the swift movement of metal mesh rushing downwards. Eventually Cole's masked face appears from below, but without any context; only motion leads us to intuit that he is in an elevator. Then confirmation: Cole rushes 'past' us, upwards; metal mesh and pipes rush downwards in a counter-shot.

The visual sequence established here, or rather the anticipated viewer response, recurs throughout the film: first confusion, then suspicion, finally confirmation. When faces (or other body parts) anticipate spaces, what you see first is the quintessence of loneliness. Wherever that person is, he is, at least until he is (we are) given a context, all alone. The experience is unsettling, anxiety-provoking. Having a context is reassuring, even if that context is itself disturbing. The scene in which the scientists first interrogate Cole begins simply with the appearance of Cole's face; it moves into the frame, seemingly out of nowhere, moving upwards from the bottom of the frame. Where is he? Until the camera reveals a row of scientists sitting behind a table, their white coats, plastic overcoats (human condoms) and stern expressions absolutely identical, we have no idea. Both the space and the people in it are disconcerting, but not nearly as unnerving as Cole's lonely face floating contextless into the frame.

Close-ups of faces obscuring spaces also feature in the airport scene at the end, where Cole's and Railly's faces, talking, then kissing, fill the screen and shut out everything and everybody else. It should feel romantic, but it doesn't; the scene is too fraught with fear, too laden with anticipated horrors. Instead it becomes another anxiety-provoking scene. For once, the viewer knows exactly where the characters are, but somehow this offers little reassurance. We know, after all, how the airport episode ends. We know that Cole and Railly, kissing in the middle of a busy airport, must be surrounded by thousands of people. But we can't see past their faces; we don't know who might be coming for them at this very moment when they have clearly let their guard down. It is the only kiss Cole and Railly share in the film, but it is a stressful moment, one that feels not like a Happy Ending but like the calm before the storm. Shortly thereafter, our worst fears are confirmed: the exchange between Cole and Jose, who presses a gun on Cole and tells him to obey orders, is shot in precisely the same way, alternating extreme close-ups of their faces and shutting out all context.

At the film's beginning and its end, the camera zooms in even further. Close-ups on faces turn into close-ups on eyes: Dr. Peters' insanely gleeful eyes as he lovingly uncaps the vial with the deadly virus and waves it beneath the custom official's nose; young Cole's eyes observing first adult Cole's death—the shot is close enough and long enough to reveal two tears, eliciting an answering smile from Railly—, then tracking the plane. Context, again, is eradicated: young Cole is with his parents, but we never see their faces.

Like extreme close-ups, distance shots and the constant alternation of high and low—of bird's-eye and frog perspective shots—serve to isolate human figures. This is established early on, when Cole makes his way to the surface. We see him struggling through a vast industrial underground complex, black as night and illuminated only by his powerful flashlight, full of pipes and puddles on the floor. The camera slowly pans to the right as Cole advances from a distance, hidden from our view by vast vats, broken piping and branches, with water gushing down from an unseen ceiling. His light blinds us more than it offers a good view of this landscape of devastation. Cut to a white surface: for a moment, we don't understand what we're looking at. Then something unseen disturbs the snow, for that is what it is, from below, and Cole removes the man-hole cover and climbs up to the street. Much of this is disorientation cinematography—once again, we initially don't know where we are or what we're looking at; we have to infer everything and await belated confirmation.

Cole emerges into a city that is likewise shown in fragments, with our view limited to whatever Cole's flashlight can pick out. Frog perspective shots show a cobweb-covered For Sale sign, dusty shoes in display cases, clothes on hangers, and the statue of an angel. We are not shown more than the absolute minimum necessary to infer that we are in a department store. Our first broader view of the store occurs in the context of a jump scare: pigeons flutter up, startling Cole; an extreme frog perspective shows them fluttering up to a hole high up in the ceiling three stories above. Cut to the outside, where we see two tilt shots, one to the right and one to the left, of a big crossroad with tall buildings on either side. Cole, seen from an extreme bird's-eye perspective, is tiny in the plaza, all alone, barely visible in the snow in his white suit. Too far away to be recognised, he looks like something crawling through the snow, less like a human being than a specimen under the microscope—or Gilliam's pinned butterfly, maybe—a fine irony, since he is himself out to collect specimens. His life, the scene implies, is worth about as much to the scientists who sent him here as that of the cockroaches and spiders he collects. And it is in constant peril: a few scenes earlier, he was threatened by a bear; an angled frog perspective immediately following the bird's-eye view of Cole in the square shows a lion roaring from the top of a tall building.

Bird's-eye and frog perspective shots spell human isolation in various ways. They dominate all interrogation scenes, where Cole on his high chair is usually filmed either from below, above, or in a slow circular panning shot, all of which convey one distinct message—he is all alone up there. Nobody is on his level. In the scene in which he is interrogated by psychiatrists in the 1990s, the camera replaces the missing high chair with contrasting angles: Cole is shot either from above or below; the doctors on the level and straight on. The more extreme the isolation, the more extreme the perspectives. Bird's-eye perspectives show Cole trapped in a hallway as orderlies of the mental institute advance upon him; then Cole is shot through a non-existent ceiling from a height of about twenty feet, manacled to a stone slab in an otherwise empty room, writhing. A fast pan upwards displays a tall building in 1990s Philadelphia, which Cole recognises as the one where a lion will roar down upon him in the future: he is in a bustling city full of people, but soon, he knows, he will be all alone in the same space. In the department store where Railly and Cole buy their clothes and wigs for their escape to the Keys, a frog perspective shot reveals an angel—the very same that Cole will see in the defunct store of the future— being hoisted up as part of the store's Christmas decoration. More than an echo or a parallel, it is an expression of anticipated loneliness in a store full of people: the plague that will wipe out the Earth's population will occur before store attendants will have a chance to take that angel down again to re-decorate for the post-Christmas season.

Perspective shots and close-ups are used to show humans alone, bereft of context, even bereft of their basic humanity, reduced to their body parts or likened to specimens in a jar or under the microscope. Loneliness is also expressed in its simplest form, as separation, through what we might call inside/out cinematography. Characters are constantly separated visually from each other, and from the viewer, by barriers like bars, cages and wire mesh. The viewer is always either on the outside looking in or on the inside looking out. Bars, wire mesh and other forms of restraint like manacles and handcuffs accompany virtually every significant scene in the film. Cole himself, Canavan notes, 'is in some form of restraint in nearly every instant he appears on screen for the first 45 minutes of *12 Monkeys*, nearly half the film'.[49] Cole's first encounter with Jeffrey Goines is partially filmed through the grey wire mesh of the ward's exit gate. The scene in which Goines offers to help him escape begins with Cole awakening at night in the mental asylum. Looking out of the window, the camera looks back at him through no less than two sets of grilles—the iron grille of the window and yet another one behind it. The act of time travel itself is repeatedly expressed by bars flitting quickly past the camera, and appropriately so: whether Cole is sent to the past or yanked back to the future, chances are that he will wake up behind bars.

Beginning with the conversation between Cole and his next-cage neighbour Jose, inmates of the future are routinely shot from the other side of a cage, indicating that there isn't enough space inside these cages to fit 'us' in there as well. These tight shots apply to the prison cells of the 1990s as well. From the perspective of a narrow hallway, the camera pans past prisoners crowded into cells, gripping bars, sitting on floors, or pacing in close-up. This, incidentally, is the only visual context that tells us that Cole has successfully arrived in the past; certainly, our first glimpse of Cole in 1990 is unlikely to convince us of this. He looks, in fact, as if he had never left—he is still naked, encased in see-through plastic, and imprisoned in a wire mesh cage. In this one, at least, there is sufficient space for Railly, who hunkers down next to Cole to interview him, with the camera alternating between over-the-shoulder shots and counter-shots. The main difference between the future and the past seems to be that cages in the past are slightly larger. As Cole is led out from the interview, the camera pans past more prison cells before passing through a steel-bar gate. This place, the viewer is given to understand, is more secure than Fort Knox. Cole is then led outside, blinking in the unfamiliar sunlight. Cut to yet more wire mesh: the next shot, showing Cole being pushed into to a grey prison van by two burly cops, is filmed from behind a wire mesh fence all the way across the street. Wire mesh and bars, in other words, do not merely dominate scenes when they have a diegetic mandate to do so; even when they don't, the camera seeks them out. The world of the past, we are told time and again, is as much a prison as the future.

Numerous critics have pointed out that the film barely distinguishes past from future.[50] Dialogue snippets and room layouts are repeated in different time frames; the same actors appear in both. All of this indicates that 'Cole's "bad future" is not to come but already here'.[51] Both future and past are dominated by cages and prison cells, dark and decaying spaces, and crumbling or peeling walls adorned with graffiti and tatty posters. The grey panels of the 1990s prison recall the grey slab stone walls in the vast interrogation room of the future. Interrogation scenes in both timelines echo one another, and the scenes in which Cole is brutally scrubbed (once in 1990, once in 2035) are visually practically identical. In 1990, his back is red from the scrubbing, mirroring the red paint scrubbed off his back in an earlier scene set in the future; in both scenes, he is surrounded by crumbling walls; in both scenes, he is forcibly turned around, leaking water from his mouth and nose. The way in which the attendant in the 1990s scene manipulates his head mirrors the scene in the future where a guard pushes his head to one side to access the bar code on the back of his neck. Shots of trees flitting past the car in which Cole and Railly travel to Philadelphia, from right to left, recall the bars racing past, from up to down, that are the film's visual hallmarks of time travel. The similarities between the pre- and post-Armageddon worlds are so pervasive that even Cole occasionally loses track of where he is. Waking up in his bed in the mental asylum in 1990, he is disoriented. Clearly thinking he is in the future collecting insect samples for the scientists, he grabs a spider from the windowsill (which he eats hastily to prevent discovery once he remembers where, or rather when, he is).

Rare outside scenes, which uniformly belong to the past and which Cole experiences as blissful, furnish the sole distinction between past and future, aside from Cole's 2035 specimen hunt early in the film. These scenes are, without exception, endowed with that sense of loss Gilliam cited. Cole's love for the Earth of the past, which he expresses ecstatically several times, is incomprehensible to its inhabitants who interpret such devotion as weird, even as proof of insanity. Sitting in a stinking cage in a smelly police station and enthusing about the fresh and germ-free air, Cole demonstrates to his observers of the 1990s what they already think anyway: this guy is as crazy as a loon. Cole on the highway, hanging his head out of the driving car's window like a happy dog on a joy-ride—'Oh, I love this air! I love to breathe this air!'; Cole in a drab winter forest, joyfully splashing around in a dirty puddle—'Oh, I love this world! And I love the frogs and spiders'—express the same disconnect. The juxtaposition is not that between the dystopian world of the future and the happy world of the past. Rather, it is the juxtaposition between Cole's 'crazy' perspective and the 'normality' experienced by the 1990s population (a group that includes Gilliam's contemporary audience). In or outside the film, normal people don't inhale fumes on the highway with ecstasy; they don't perceive the stunning scenery Cole sees in a dreary woodland somewhere between Baltimore and Philadelphia. There is no love lost between these normal people and the Earth they inhabit. There is only the 'proliferation of atomic devices' and the 'pollution of land, sea and air' that Dr. Peters lists to a distracted Railly as part of the catalogue of human sins sure to lead straight to the apocalypse. Whether in the past or in the future, Cole is the only person capable of seeing the lost past through the eyes of love, the only person who can perceive a stunning landscape where others would merely see muck and undergrowth.

In fact, in the reality of 'normal' people and therefore also in the film's cinematographic reality, stunning landscapes or cityscapes don't exist. They are, without exception, banished to the world of fiction. Where such fictional landscapes are shown, they are inevitably filmed straight-on, in marked contrast to the usual tilted angles that dominate the film's reality. All are slow-reveal scenes leading us, gradually but inevitably, from the beautiful world of fiction back to harsh reality. The camera lovingly lingers on, then slowly pans out from inside a beautiful plaza framed by Grecian columns, a handsome castello in the background and blue mountains behind it. Unmoving figures in eighteenth-century costumes in the plaza define this beautiful space as a painting. As the camera pulls back to reveal the frame, leaving us visually to linger in what is most likely eighteenth-century Florence, a header script informs us that we are really in 'Baltimore, April 1990'. The camera then pulls further back beyond painting and frame until a female speaker's face appears on the left—we are at the lecture attended by Railly—and the painting blurs into the background.

Such slow-reveal scenes of bogus beauty occur repeatedly, usually in more traumatic contexts. In the mental institute, a lingering close-up shot of the TV ad for the Florida Keys shows a glorious sunset over an ocean with a man and a woman standing in the shallows, kissing. From there, with the camera still steady on the asylum's TV screen, we are flung back into black and white—the programme has switched to the Marx Brothers' *Monkey Business*. The camera pulls back, stranding us, with Cole, in the asylum. The third and possibly most traumatic scene of this nature features a long-held shot of a beautiful landscape showing mountains, trees and a lake in glorious hues of orange, brown and blue. A slow pan to the left, and Cole's profile appears. From the bottom of the screen, the faces of the scientists rise into view, crooning an enthusiastic if out-of-tune chorus of 'Blueberry Hill', Cole's favourite song. Cole, then, is back in the future, still manacled to a bed, still surrounded by supervision cameras, videos, screens and other machinery, still surrounded by scientists in white coats and human condoms, and still offered a second-hand, cheapened experience—the tuneless song, the painted landscape—in place of the real thing. Nothing has changed, yet he is informed that everything is different now: he is not in a prison but in a hospital. In fact, he is being rewarded for having identified Leland Goines' laboratory as the origin of the virus. His rewards are a full pardon, which is waved under his nose, the tone-deaf rendition of the song, and the only two things in the room endowed with any colour: Cole's usual grey army-issue blanket has been replaced by a child's duvet on which teddy bears cavort in the snow, and the landscape painting has been affixed right above his bed, where he is sure to see it as soon as he opens his eyes.

The film's method of juxtaposing fictional and real spaces is always the same. Steady close-ups of intense beauty—the Florida Keys, eighteenth-century Florence, the spectacular forest and the glittering sea that furnish the background for James Stewart and Kim Novak—fill the screen for protracted moments. Even if we know that this is fiction, which we always do—from the flicker of the TV or movie screens, from the costumes and stillness of the figures in the Florence square, from our immediate recognition of Hitchcock's actors—the reprieve from reality's unrelenting ugliness, darkness and colourlessness is intense. The effect, inevitably, is one of profound disappointment. Relief is first offered and then snatched away. But these scenes also express an alignment with Cole's viewpoint, a momentary and vicarious experience of Cole's reality-denial at the end of the film. Even perfectly aware that these scenes of beauty are not real, we want to stay there, just as Cole, knowing that the world of the past cannot endure, wants to live there forever, however long that may be.

Finally, the juxtaposition of fictional and real spaces serves as yet another visualisation of Cole's essential loneliness. He is alone in the past, the only person on the planet able to perceive its beauty. And he is alone in the future, the only person who, seduced by the imperceptible and unappreciated beauty of an unloved world, refuses to bow to the dictate of determinism.

Footnotes

40. Gilliam cited in Bob McCabe, *Dark Knights*, p. 169.
41. On names and naming in *12 Monkeys*, see Canavan, '"You can't change anything"', p. 94.
42. Ashbrook, *The Pocket Essential Terry Gilliam*, p. 74.
43. Gilliam's comment is quoted in Ashbrook, *The Pocket Essential Terry Gilliam*, p. 73.
44. Gilliam in Christie, *Gilliam on Gilliam*, p. 230.
45. Beecroft is cited and discussed in Calhoun, '12 Monkeys', pp. 36 and 34 respectively, the quotation on p. 34.
46. Quoted and discussed in Ruben, '*12 Monkeys*', p. 323.
47. Calhoun, '12 Monkeys', p. 36.
48. Gilliam in Christie, *Gilliam on Gilliam*, p. 227. On Gilliam's choice of location, see also Bob McCabe, *Dark Knights*, pp. 164-5.
49. Canavan, '"You can't change anything"', p. 95.
50. For example, in Fry and Craig, 'A Carnival of Apes', pp. 5-7.
51. Canavan, '"You can't change anything"', p. 95.

6. Free Will, Determinism and Doing What You're Told

'All of [Gilliam's] films are about liberty,' Aldersey-Williams has claimed: 'The recurrent themes of make-believe kingdoms and time travel are merely devices for exploring this idea.'[52] In *12 Monkeys*, time travel is the secondary device for exploring the idea of liberty. The primary one is the juxtaposition between free will and determinism, and here is where *12 Monkeys* seems to be caught in something of a bind. On the one hand, it proposes that the world of the 1990s can't be brought back from the brink of apocalypse because, as Cole repeatedly states, 'This already happened'. The future, he tells us over and over, is written and cannot be changed. On the other hand, the unchangeability of the future does not dent the scientists' project of finding the original virus and developing a cure for themselves, since both their hope in the success of the venture and their fear of its failure imply the possibility of a changed future. Time travel in *12 Monkeys* is one-directional: the scientists only ever send people into the past, never into their own future to see if their plan will pan out. Thus the scientists are as blind to their own future as the citizens of the 1990s are to their imminent destruction. It is this blindness that enables the illusion that the future is wide open.

Our ability to believe in free will is thus clearly dependent on our concept of time. If linear time is an illusion—as per Einstein, Minkowski, McTaggart and others—the future already exists, which implies a deterministic universe. And yet *12 Monkeys* seems to suggest that it is possible to influence the future, an idea entirely reliant on the illusion of linear time. Denizens of the 1990s live in a deterministic universe (after all, 'This already happened') whereas the scientists of the future are apparently able to exercise their free will and influence their future. Both cannot be true. Either linear time—and with it the possibility of changing future events—exists or it doesn't. The laws of the universe don't change just because it has aged by another 45 years.

At first glance, the idea of free will seems to be incompatible with a deterministic universe, for if free will could result in changes to the future, those changes might also affect cosmological laws, which are immutable: 'It is difficult to reconcile the intuitive evidence that conscious decisions are causally effective with the view that the physical world can be explained to operate perfectly by physical law.'[53] Much of the thinking on free will has thus dedicated itself to the development of a theory of free will that is not in conflict with the laws of nature. Compatibilists hold, as the moniker suggests, that free will and determinism are compatible. Yet this can only be achieved by relegating free will to the realm of personal belief: humans believe that they have free will, but they could be wrong (just as their belief in linear time could be mistaken).[54] Freedom of will, in other words, does not result in freedom of action; even with the best (free) will in the world, you have no influence on the future. Incompatibilists, conversely, arrive at the opposite conclusion (that free will is incompatible with determinism) by way of the same argument, namely, that free will is illusory.[55] To them, all choices are oblivious to their choosers, and all have already been made.

The debate between compatibilists and incompatibilists, who despite their incompatible monikers seem to hold perfectly compatible views, centres on a failure to distinguish between that which is *known* and that which is *real*. To illustrate: let us assume, for the moment, that what we 'know' to be real actually corresponds to an objective reality. Let us further assume that free will exists; that is, that it can be the cause of an action that results in an effect. If we draw a knowledge line between them, that line would parallel a linear timeline, like this:

Known (and therefore real)	Known (and therefore real)	Unknown (and therefore open to various possibilities)
Past	Present	Future
Free Will	Cause	Action/Effect

Yet this is precisely what some philosophers have denied. 'Experience teaches us no less clearly than reason', writes Spinoza, 'that men believe themselves free, simply because they are conscious of their actions, and unconscious of the causes whereby those actions are determined.'[56] Spinoza's knowledge line, then, would look like this:

Known (and therefore real)	Known (and therefore real)	Unknown (and therefore open to various possibilities)
Past	Present	Future
Free Will	Action/Effect	Cause

If we accept Spinoza's reasoning and further assume that all humans must operate within the illusion of a linear timeline (for they are aware of past and present, but unaware of the future), the claim of free will to objective reality is no better than that of linear time. For if free will were real, it would have to either change the past or violate the laws of nature. Effect cannot precede cause.

Both compatibilists and incompatibilists seem to claim that free will is an illusion, born of our belief in linear time and a strong desire for freedom and control. Even those who presume that free will exists are careful to distinguish between freedom of will and freedom of action. Free will is, according to compatibilists, all in our heads, which does not seem all that far from the incompatibilistic position that free will is an illusion. If philosophers have maintained that even the free-est of will may not result in freedom of action, dystopian novelists, from Huxley's *Brave New World* (1932) onward, have held the opposite: the existence of freedom of action in the absence of free will. Humans, they claim,

> have a great deal of everyday freedom to do whatever we wanted, yet our freedom of *will* would be severely limited. We would be free to *act* or to choose *what* we willed, but we would not have the ultimate power over what it is that we willed. Other persons would be pulling the strings, not by coercing or forcing us to do things against our wishes, but by manipulating us into having the wishes they wanted us to have.[57]

If humans are endowed with free will coupled with the inability to enact it, determinism is real. If human freedom of action exists but is made meaningless by an inability to will that action freely, then 'determinism poses no real threat to free will, or at least to any kind of freedom or will "worth wanting"'.[58] Threat or not, determinism is generally understood as free will's polar opposite and as such has become a key concept in the history of thought. So far philosophers have identified, to name just a few: biological determinism (which holds that behaviours and beliefs are determined by genetics and biochemical conditions); theological determinism (the idea that a creator deity either decrees every possible outcome or knows all of them in advance); cultural determinism (the claim that behaviour is determined by cultural context); logical determinism (the idea that all propositions about past, present or future must be either true or false, and that thus whatever happens in the future is decreed by what is already determined to be either true or false in the present), and the one that would have interested Einstein: causal determinism. Unlike Einstein, however, most of us are unable to imagine cause and consequence without resorting to linear time, as the following explanations, distilled from a long history of philosophy on the concepts of free will and determinism, show (all emphases added):

> Causal determinism holds that everything is caused by *prior* conditions, making it impossible for anything else to happen. [...] Causal determinism proposes that there is an unbroken chain of *prior* occurrences *stretching back* to the origin of the universe. [It is] the notion *that the past and the present dictate the future* entirely and necessarily by rigid natural laws, that every occurrence results inevitably from *prior events*.[59]

Even the debunking of an illusion (free will) is only thinkable by recourse to another illusion (linear time). Free will, as it turns out, has quite a few things in common with linear time. Just like the Theory of Special Relativity denies the objective reality of linear time, the reality of free will (or at least its ability to influence the future) is repudiated by many philosophers, both those who claim that free will is compatible with determinism and those who claim that it isn't.

And yet, just like the belief in linear time, faith in free will, usually coupled with the idea that it equates with freedom of action, is practically a cultural given in Western societies. The reason for this is quite simply that both linear time and free will are highly *intuitive*. They are clearly linked, since only our inability to see into the future enables us to accept free will as true. But we rely on this truth for other reasons as well. Unlike our belief in linear time, our acceptance of free will has a bearing on our understanding of both freedom and morality; it defines how we see ourselves as humans. A study conducted by Nichols and Knobe in 2007 found that the vast majority of respondents held that the universe is indeterministic and that moral responsibility is incompatible with determinism.[60] Various other studies have shown that those whose belief in free will had been weakened—for example by exposure to literature arguing against free will—were more likely to lie, cheat, engage in aggressive behaviour and felt less guilty about their transgressions against others. They were also less able to engage in counterfactual thinking (the ability to say 'If I had acted differently...') and thus less able to question and learn from their own decisions, including those that had harmed others.[61] It seems, then, that just like our belief in linear time enables us to make sense of our physical world, our faith in free will enables us to navigate our social world. Whether or not these ideas have a basis in objective reality, their effect on human behaviour is profound.

Causality and Determinism

If, as I have argued earlier, *12 Monkeys* rejects the reality of linear time, then it must also reject the possibility of changing the future through individual action —both for the hopelessly doomed inhabitants of the past and the hopeful scientists of the future. The easiest way to square this with the scientists' hopes of finding a cure for the virus is simply to assume that they, who get so many things wrong, are wrong about this as well. They may wrongly believe they have free will and that it equates with freedom of action, giving them the power to influence the future. Given their demonstrable difficulties in negotiating the past, we may be persuaded that their grasp on the future is no better. Unaware of the paradox, they may look upon the 'dying world' of the past from a deterministic viewpoint while assuming that their own future is open to various possibilities. In their mad pursuit of a cure, they may have forgotten that the same laws of nature govern both pre- and post-Apocalyptic time.

While this is certainly thinkable, it seems a simplistic explanation for a film that does not shy away from complexity. We might, then, follow it down the rabbit hole once again and consider the scientists' paradoxical project in light of a concept that impacts both cosmology and philosophy, both time and free will: causal determinism. To Gilliam, in fact, determinism was not only the central aspect of his film but his main reason for making it:

> If your going back in time has always been predetermined, then you have always been there. You don't have a choice in the matter. You might think you have a choice, but you're going to go back in time and you will be part of that event. I think *Twelve Monkeys* is very Oriental in that sense—that's why I did the wheel of the monkeys going round for the poster design. It's trying to break out of it, but it's a wheel that keeps going round. And that's one of the things that attracted me to it, that the kid is always going to see himself die. Then he's going to grow up and the world is going to be decimated, he's going to break the law and end up in prison, and it's going to go on and on and on. Just this wheel turning and turning. It has this predestination. [...] That to me was an important part of why I wanted to do it.[62]

Numerous hints throughout *12 Monkeys* define the film on Gilliam's terms, as a profoundly deterministic work. One of them is the recurring use of characters from folk literature and mythology. Chicken Little is awarded an honourable mention, as is, of course, Cassandra, both in ways that define their dire prophecies not as fantastical but as fact. Prometheus, who stole fire from the gods and was punished for it with eternal torture, appears in Leland Goines' dinner speech as a warning against human overreach. The professor whose lecture Railly attends in her first scene quotes Omar Khayyam's most deterministic lines and moreover links, as Gilliam does, determinism with time: 'Yesterday, this day's madness did prepare / Tomorrow's silence, triumph or despair.' And finally, religion, that greatest mouthpiece of determinism of all, plays a significant symbolic role in the film. The scientists can easily be read as 'both God and Antichrist', simultaneously 'condemning' the Earth and trying to 'redeem' it.[63] Cole himself can be read with equal ease as a Christ-figure.[64] James Cole and Jesus Christ share the same initials. Both play the double role of prophet and dutiful son (with the voice in Cole's head possibly doubling as 'a meagre sort of holy ghost').[65] Both lead a monastic life and wear white robes (or are shown naked and bleeding) as they go through their trials. Both are subject to temptation as they approach death (Cole's wild determination to live in the permanent present is his version of the

Garden of Gethsemane). Both are finally martyred. 'This martyrdom seems confirmed by the way that J.C. falls to his death', Lashmet points out. 'James Cole slowly leans forward with arms outspread but elbows bent, as if being gently lowered from a crucifix by time itself. In case this is too subtle, Gilliam actually depicts Cole wearing a personalized T-shirt that says "Chris..." (with the rest of the letters obscured by a sweater).'[66] Lashmet has even proposed that young Cole may have come away from the airport with more than just a future lifetime of nightmares: he may also have obtained antibodies to the virus. After all, just like everyone else at the airport, he was exposed; unlike everybody else, he survived. Thus, just as Jesus is the Christian believer's way to Heaven, 'James Cole himself may be the cure. This makes his assassination all the more tragic and his divine status all the more clear.'[67] Such interpretations, while acknowledging determinism, also attempt to inject hope into a hopeless situation, to square the deterministic circle. If Cole is predestined to die, there is no way of saving him or humanity; there is only, as Gilliam put it, 'this wheel turning and turning'.

Gilliam has said repeatedly that 'the Americans in particular had a hard time accepting that'.[68] How hard a time is demonstrated in two major threads of *12 Monkeys* scholarship: the 'If-Only' strand and the Great Irony Tradition. The first proposes that the future *could* have been saved if only people had recognised that Cole is the cure, or if only the scientists had sent someone back in time to throttle Dr. Peters in his crib before he grew up to become that deadly combo of virologist and apocalypse nut.[69] The second suggests that, irony of ironies, it is actually Cole and Railly's attempt to *prevent* the apocalypse that causes it.[70] The smoking gun is Railly's warning to Leland Goines about the impending theft of the virus, which leads to Leland Goines' decision to strengthen security protocols by surrendering vital computer codes to his assistant—Dr. Peters. Railly is only spurred into action because of Cole, and Cole is only spurred into action because he's been sent back in time in order to prevent the worst. 'Significantly', the Great-Irony conclusion has it, 'had they done *nothing at all* the virus would never have been released.'[71] All of these interpretations are convincing in different contexts, and yet none of them can stop the wheel of determinism from just turning and turning. 'If-only' fails because it relies on the linearity of time and the idea that you can go back and fix it. Great Irony fails because, as Leland Goines makes clear after Railly's call, he wants his security protocols upgraded to prevent unauthorised access to the virus. But *unauthorised* access is not the problem. As Goines is on the phone with Railly, assuring her 'that neither my son nor any other unauthorised person has access to potentially dangerous organisms in my laboratory', we can see Dr. Peters in the background, working away on a computer, presumably on the very virus under discussion. The follow-up conversation between Goines and Peters establishes that whatever extra security measures Goines wants applied, he will rely on Dr. Peters to implement. The implication is clear: Peters' access to the virus was already authorised and absolute before Railly's call. Railly's warning, in other words, neither causes or prevents the apocalypse; it is as irrelevant as the unused antibodies in Cole's blood.

The reasons why we cannot square the deterministic circle is as obvious as the reasons why we keep trying. The first is explained, as Gilliam has illustrated with his circle of monkeys, by the link between non-linear time ('If your going back in time has always been predetermined, then you have always been there') and determinism ('You don't have a choice in the matter'). The second is explained by the link between determinism and dystopia. We *might* come around to the idea that we have neither free will nor freedom of action—we might even accept that the future is set in stone because, given the non-linearity of time, it already exists—if that future wasn't so unspeakably appalling. This immediately raises the question: does it *have* to be? To which *12 Monkeys* seems to respond: yes, it does. For the principle that governs the world of the film is not time but causality. Causality, however, must be calculable to produce a predictable effect. Because causality embodies calculability, it negates free will and breeds oppression. Thus causal determinism will always result in a dystopian future.

Unlike the film's portrayal of time, its idea of causality differs slightly from its scientific model. In Einstein's thinking, the order of causally-linked events is never in doubt: effect always follows cause. It is impossible to see the window breaking before the boy kicks the ball into it. This is precisely why causality is the only objective reality: because all observers, while disagreeing on the time elapsed between two events and the space between them, will agree on their sequence. Thus time is not responsible for causality: causality is responsible for time. *12 Monkeys* adopts these ideas for its own purposes. Time in the film is not a direct line leading from past to present to future but a never-ending loop where things are their own causes. Cole's death as an adult causes his childhood trauma of watching a man die (without realising that the man is his future self) which causes the scientists' decision to send him 'back' in time, a decision that, in turn, causes his death at the airport. It is not, strictly speaking, an Einsteinian model—for nothing in Einstein's universe can be either uncaused or the cause of itself—but it does adopt Einstein's most principal insight: that that which constitutes reality is not time but events.

Causal determinism as the philosophical basis for *12 Monkeys*' reality would explain rather a lot. Causality dictates that there can be no such thing as a 'free will' that results in freedom of action, because all events, whether 'past' or 'future', already exist. Thus, the film, unusually for a time-travel movie, must propose the immutability of events and the insignificance of time. Because causality, not time, matters, Cole's job is not to save the world from disaster. The scientists confirm this with their scornful disinterest in 'that dying world', and Cole too confirms it, too insistently to be ignored, when he says time and again that his mission 'won't help you... won't change anything'. So far, so obvious.

Less obviously, though, causal determinism is also the reason for the inevitability of dystopia. In Cole's dystopian future, there is no such thing as 'your mission, should you choose to accept it': Cole once inadvertently points this out when he remarks innocently that he didn't volunteer for volunteer duty. But causal determinism is more than the absence of free will and freedom of action; it is the principle of a cause yielding an inevitable and thus calculable result. As such, causality, of necessity, breeds oppression. Cole's words at the airport, uttered as Jose presses the gun into his hands, contain a partial recognition of this: 'This part isn't about the virus at all, is it? It's about following orders. About doing what you're told.' Any effect is only as calculable as its cause, and the film's most central scenes show us that both are eminently calculable. If you try to go through airport security with a suitcase full of vials containing unknown substances, you will be stopped and asked to open the case. It is a cause-and-effect sequence that Dr. Peters can absolutely rely upon: this is how he launches the virus. If your wanted-poster is already in the hands of every security officer at the airport and you then try to run through airport security, gun drawn and aimed at another person, you will be shot. It is a cause-and-effect sequence that the scientists can absolutely rely upon. This is how Cole, who thinks his job is to shoot Dr. Peters, fulfills his actual two-fold mission. By pointing the gun at Peters, he identifies him to the scientists as the carrier of the virus; by dying and watching himself die, he identifies *himself* to the scientists as the sole surviving observer of the virus launch and thus as the ideal person—'a good observer'—to be sent back in time to find the original virus. Causal determinism is thus far more than the absence of free will and freedom of action (although it clearly comprises both), it is is the underlying principle of the film's dystopia. The contaminated and uninhabitable planet surface; the dictatorial scientists in charge of an imprisoned humanity; the Permanent Emergency Code that justifies stiff prison sentences for non-crimes like the 'insolence, defiance, disregard of authority' for which Cole is serving 25-to-life: all of it makes sense if we recognise the causality of events, and with it the total calculability of effects, as the only existing reality. As surely as effect follows cause, reality never changes, just as Hitchcock's movie never does: the only thing that changes is our observation of it. You cannot will reality, freely or otherwise; and you cannot change it. All you can do is observe it. And this is, of course, the purpose of Cole's Christ-like sacrifice: in sending Cole to the slaughter, the scientists merely ensure that they get the best view of this particular cause-and-effect sequence, a front-row seat on a reality that was always going to unfold in this way and no other.

The Cinematography of Determinism: Colours

12 Monkeys engages in what we could call cinematographic determinism by assigning each timeline a strict colour scheme, or, rather, a *colourlessness* scheme. Roger Pratt, the film's cinematographer, pointed out 'that color was used sparingly but selectively throughout the film, to provide a series of psychological "signposts" for the audience. "Mainly, I think one could say we focused on things that had had the color drained out of them".'[72] Cole's future is a world of relentless blacks, whites and greys. Pitch-black subterranean spaces alternate with grey interrogation rooms; the Earth's surface is a cluttered-yet-empty world covered in blinding snow. The colour-palette of the 1990s barely distinguishes past from future. Upon arrival, Cole is flung into a grey cage in a grey police station, then transported in a grey prison van into a mental hospital with peeling white stucco walls, white tiles, white bar gates and white bedding, a place where he is dressed in white pyjamas and a white robe and surrounded by doctors in white coats and attendants in white T-shirts (Figure 8).

Figure 8: Cole and Goines (Brad Pitt) in the white world of the loony bin

The room in which the psychiatrists interrogate Cole to assess his mental fitness is held in the same hues. A slow and threatening frog's eye pan reveals a vast room that, although bright, is the opposite of cheery. It is largely empty, oversized and sparsely furnished, with a shiny-white linoleum floor and a white-tiled wall. Cole is in white, his wardens are in white, the hospital's doctors, lined up behind a table like the scientists of the future, are clad in white. As they interrogate him, the camera repeatedly focuses on a front left close-up of a white thermos coffee pot and mugs. Even the TV in the asylum is predominantly black and white; only the Florida Keys commercial is shot through with a bit of colour, a dirty ochre that poses unsuccessfully as a glorious orange sunset. In the night-time dormitory scene, what little light there is reveals white walls, a white table and chair in the centre of the room, white metal bedframes, white bedding and pyjamas—and, of course, grey and white grille covering the windows. The room in which Cole is confined after his temporary escape from the ward is nearly square with a small grey floor space and very high ceilings. Twenty-foot-tall walls in a dirty washed-out grey colour that may once have been white, adorned with absolutely nothing, stretch upwards towards the camera; in the centre of the room, there is a grey slab of stone on which Cole is manacled in his white pyjamas. He awakens on a different stone slab, in a room that sports the same limited floor space and the same intimidating ceiling height. Only its slightly darker greyish tint tells us that he is now back in the future. No wonder Cole cannot keep his timelines separate, as he demonstrates when he catches and then swallows the spider in 1990: all timelines look more or less the same.

All inside or outside spaces in the film that are diegetically presented as real (as opposed to fictional) are assigned a specific palette of gloomy colours. The World War I sequences are staged in a dirty olive green, sporting greenish poison gas and grey uniforms that appear olive green in the light of the shell fire. The hotel room in which Cole and Railly rest up on their way to Philadelphia is decorated in drab beiges and browns, with the bathroom tiled in matching beige. The woods through which Cole runs are uniformly brown without a touch of greenery, interspersed with flecks of dirty snow. The airport is a greyed-out space where everything appears fuzzy and indistinct. With its grey walls, grey escalators, and a warehouse-type ceiling with plastic or glass panelling letting in some light, it is yet another symphony of colourlessness. Colours other than the interminable blacks, whites, greys and browns appear only rarely. They flash past quickly and are gone again, emphasising the dreary surroundings rather than offering relief from them—a red ball here, a pair of green rubber boots there. More often, non-monochromes are relegated to the world of fiction: the glorious colours of the landscape mounted above Cole's bed; the washed-out colours of the Florida Keys commercial; the pleasant impressionistic hues of the painting showing the Florence square; the fake greenery in the headquarters of the Army of the 12 Monkeys. Colours are inevitably unmasked as the products of either imagination or imitation; the film's diegetic reality is colourless.

In this reality, individuals disappear. Cole in his clear-and-white latex suit is invisible in the snowy landscape; he fades against the grey stone wall in the interrogation room. In the dark subterranean warehouse that he traverses on his way to the surface, blinding us with his flashlight, we cannot make him out at all. In 1990, he again dissolves against the white walls of the hospital in his white robe and white pyjamas. In a monochrome world, individuals can neither stand out from their surroundings nor be distinguished from one another. Sinister little jokes keep pointing this out to us. The reason Cole escapes so easily from the mental hospital is that the guard mistakes him, an inmate in a white robe, for a doctor in a white coat. In the dormitory scene,

Jeffrey Goines jumps from bed to bed, ripping open a pillow and screeching like a monkey, until the inmates are covered in white feathers, absolutely indistinguishable from one another. The film's most colourful and obtrusive characters, the only people who really get themselves noticed, are the bums and doomsday criers in the streets, and these are also naturally the ones from whom normal people avert their eyes, doing their best to pretend that they're not there. Fading into the background, we are told again and again, denotes normality; standing out in any way is shorthand for either insanity or criminality. This is confirmed again when Railly and Cole are chased by the Philadelphia police shortly after escaping from the hotel room in which a bum hits Railly in the face and Cole breaks the teeth from his mouth. Holding handkerchiefs to their faces, she to her bleeding nose, he to his bleeding mouth, she tells him, apparently without a trace of irony, 'Try to blend in.' This is Gilliam at his wacky best—we are reminded of the bizarre scene in which the scientists serenade Cole with 'Blueberry Hill'—but of course Railly's instruction is not merely a pun but also a comment on determinism. In a world where blending in is synonymous with sanity and legitimacy, everyone either does or tries to. Attracting notice—by, say, proclaiming the End of Days to a bunch of psychiatrists charged with assessing your mental state, or when the cops are after you and your face suddenly appears on a giant screen behind you—will land you behind bars in short order. Best, then, to blend in: a tiny white figure barely discernible in a snowy landscape; naked in the woods, your dirty skin perfectly camouflaged by brown mud and undergrowth; a grey figure in a grey cage, side by side with thousands of others; decked out in a white robe in a white room behind the bars of a white gate, surrounded by doctors in white coats and orderlies in white T-shirts… to the point of invisibility.

Where all colours are the same, all people are the same. Colourlessness is the cinematographic language of determinism because individuals blend in, fade into the background, disappear into their world. That such people could have any control over shaping their world or determining its course is a ludicrous proposition.

Footnotes

52. Aldersey-Williams, 'Terry Gilliam', p. 98.
53. Legare, 'The Question of Free Will', p. 264.
54. For some of these theories, see Caruso, *Free Will and Consciousness.*
55. There are some very interesting exceptions to this; see, for example, Yu's article on Kant's incompatibilism.
56. Spinoza, *Ethics*, p. 54.
57. Kane, *A Contemporary Introduction to Free Will*, p. 2, emphases original.
58. Kane, *A Contemporary Introduction to Free Will*, p. 7.
59. From the Wikipedia articles on 'Determinism' (https://en.wikipedia.org/wiki/Determinism) and 'Free Will' (https://en.wikipedia.org/wiki/Free_will).
60. Nichols and Knobe, 'Moral Responsibility and Determinism.'
61. Studies conducted by Kathleen Vohs and Roy Baumeister; see the work by Vohs and Schooler and Baumeister, Masicampo and DeWall respectively.
62. Gilliam in Bob McCabe, *Dark Knights*, p. 170.
63. Rosen, *Apocalyptic Transformation*, p. 87.
64. For example in Lashmet, '"The Future is History"', 63-4.
65. Lashmet, '"The Future is History"', p. 64.
66. Lashmet, '"The Future is History"', p. 63.
67. Lashmet, '"The Future is History"', p. 70.
68. Gilliam in Bob McCabe, *Dark Knights*, p. 170.
69. For example, Canavan, '"You can't change anything"', p. 100; Greenberg, '*12 Monkeys*', p. 127.
70. For example, Canavan, '"You can't change anything"', and Greenberg, '*12 Monkeys*', p. 127.
71. Canavan, '"You can't change anything"', p. 100, emphasis original.
72. Roger Pratt's remark is quoted and discussed in Pizzello, '*Twelve Monkeys*', p. 39.

7. Strangers on a Plane: On Not Answering the Big Question

The film's penultimate scene deserves a brief discussion on its own because so many commentators have seen it as the only glimmer of hope. It shows Dr. Peters taking his seat on the plane, about to embark on his virus distribution tour around the world. As he settles in, stashing the carry-on case with the virus underneath his seat, we hear the voice of an as yet unseen woman next to him: 'It's obscene. All the violence, all the lunacy. Shootings even at airports now.' As Peters leans back in his seat, the camera pans back to reveal the speaker to be the lead scientist from the future (Carol Florence). 'One might say that we're the next endangered species,' she continues: 'Human beings.' Peters, still breathing heavily from running, agrees entirely: 'I think you're right, Ma'am. I think you've hit the nail on the head.' She introduces herself, offering a handshake: 'Jones is my name. I'm in insurance.'

To me, this seems a rather ominous statement, given that insurance is not something you actually need unless the worst has already happened. Yet viewers without number have interpreted this scene as the usual 'hope-for-the-future' statement of the traditional apocalypse movie. She is 'Insuring against her world being forever subterranean. Possibly insuring against ours actually dying!'[73] If the scientist boards the plane to stop the further spread of the virus, some have proclaimed optimistically, then this would imply that the scientists of the future will do better for humanity than those of our present: 'The work of virologists provides the means to wipe out the human population of the planet, but scientists from the future potentially can create a cure.'[74] Or maybe, in a slight variation on the theme, the scientist's job is to save what remains of the world: 'the audience understands that Cole's mission has succeeded, allowing those in 2035 to locate the virus in its pure form and find an antidote.'[75] At the very least, the scene on the plane gives us an emotional break after two hours of doom and gloom: '[T]his coda is supposed to ensure that Cole's death has not been in vain. The female scientist who, in the last scene, sits next to the "bad guy" on the plane—who, aptly enough, is in the "insurance" business—continues Cole's redemptive task and, in a sense, confers some purpose on his death.'[76]

Is this, then, the answer to the Big Question? Is the world saved or lost? Does Gilliam, after subjecting us to more than two hours of hopelessness, colourlessness and determinism, throw us a bone at the very end?

First of all, we should remind ourselves that this is not the very end. It is the film's penultimate scene, followed by the bird's-eye shot of young Cole getting in the car and the close-up of his eyes as they follow a plane—presumably the one that will carry the virus to the next major city. The fact that the scene on the plane is not actually the final scene deprives it of much of the clout that it might have had as the film's 'message-bearer'. Gilliam has, in fact, hinted at this when he stated that he wanted the film to end with the plane scene and only inserted what is now the final scene after a lengthy argument with producer Chuck Roven, who 'wanted me to show that the boy had been changed by the experience of what he saw at the airport'. In the end, though, Gilliam came around to the idea, admitting that 'this ludicrously extravagant shot which I only set up to piss the producer off worked beautifully': 'It's just connecting the circle a bit more, so you see the boy watching the plane flying overhead which is actually (spoiler alert) the salvation of the future.'[77]

So there it is, finally, our answer to the Big Question: the future *is* saved. And yet, instead of wallowing in the relief this supposedly provides, the mysterious plane scene seems to have bothered viewers a great deal. At any rate, it keeps coming up in interviews with Gilliam:

Q: There's been a lot of discussion regarding *Twelve Monkeys* about the insurance woman at the end. Was the intention of that scene to close any ambiguities in the movie? Or should the ambiguities remain open?

A: I think there are several ambiguities, but the intention was in our minds, there was no question that she was the scientist from the future. My reading of the whole thing is that she gets the virus with which she is able to go back to the future and eventually save the future. Five billion people still die—all that's necessary. So it was a very long-term solution!!!

Quite honestly, I like the fact there's all of this discussion. [...] Certainly our intention was that she is the scientist. She does get the virus and she goes back to the future and somehow allows the future generations of her generation to eventually reclaim the earth.[78]

There it is again, the answer to the Big Question, straight from the horse's mouth. So why should we argue with him? One reason is that Gilliam's answer couches the matter not in authoritative terms but as a matter of perspective ('the intention was in our minds...'; 'My reading of the whole thing is...'; 'Certainly our intention was...'). Readings, however, can be flawed, and ambiguities have a way of undercutting intentions. Elsewhere, Gilliam cautiously points out that no matter what his intentions, he has no interpretive ownership of the end product:

I'm not proprietorial about the films; once they're done they belong to anyone who wants to watch them, and each person who watches creates a different film in their watching of it. [...] I know exactly what everything means—or at least, what I intended it to mean. As I went along, it all made sense to me and I argued it through with David [Peoples], but that doesn't mean there aren't a hundred different versions of the film out there.[79]

The film he intended to make, then, may not be the one we see. To cite Jeffrey Goines: 'There's no right, there's no wrong, there's only popular opinion.' Or perhaps Cole: 'The movie never changes—it can't change—but every time you see it, it seems different because you're different. You see different things.' Were we to accept Gilliam's intention that the scientists 'eventually save the future' as the film's reality, the Big Question would be answered for good. But maybe it merely shifts meaning: perhaps the Big Question becomes whether saving the future is actually a vision of hope.

Before we consider this, however, we should take our leave of the most hopeful interpretation of all: that Madame Scientist wants to get her hands on the unadulterated virus in order to save the past, i.e. to contain the breakout in 1996. The idea is incompatible with the film's understanding of events as real and linear time as illusory. The scientist is not there to stop the further spread of the virus, just as Cole's job was never to stop its release, but to gather information. In dying, he has succeeded. Madame Scientist now knows whom Cole was trying to shoot and thus who is the carrier of the original virus, the basis for a potential vaccine. On the plane, she is closer to it than ever; in fact, she has probably contracted it through the handshake.

Instead of hope for 'that dying world', the scene seems to offer a final comment on the free will versus determinism dilemma. Free will, such as the decision to send Cole back in time, clearly exists. And yet, the decision to stop the virus does not, or not in the sense that the will to do so could result in freedom of action, since this would presume the existence of linear time. Such a decision would occasion a paradox loop: if Cole went back in time and stopped the virus, the world would be saved, and therefore the situation in which he would be sent back to the past would not even arise. Since the future does not occur 'after' the past but already exists, nothing can change it. And yet—and this may well be the extent of free will—you still have to make a decision to let it take its course. Free will and determinism in the film are thus not alternatives. Humans may perceive them as contradictions in terms, just as they perceive time as linear. Yet both free will and determinism have to occur to enable the causality of events. Much like linear time, the dichotomy between free will and determinism is thus unmasked as a false premise, as something that is dependent entirely on perspective and unrelated to any reality.

So much, then, for saving the past. But what about Gilliam's ideas about the future? 'My reading of the whole thing is that she gets the virus with which she is able to go back to the future and eventually save the future', he says. But is this actually a vision of hope? We don't even have to take up Gilliam's explicit invitation to quibble with his 'reading of the whole thing'. We merely need to wonder what it actually means to 'save the future'. What it seems to mean is that 'the medical overlords are allowing the death of billions in order to assure their later ascendancy'.[80] What it means is that Madame Scientist and her colleagues will 'rule what remains of the world',[81] cementing, in the process, their tyranny over others 'whom they basically use as experimental animals'.[82] In essence, we are asked to accept as a positive that humanity's survival must be purchased with the coin of human misery stretching far into the post-apocalyptic future.

If we accept Gilliam's reading, then 'scientists from the future potentially can create a cure'.[83] For the virus, perhaps. But not for what actually ails the world. Not for our inability to see beyond the present moment; not for our tendency to class anyone whose viewpoint differs radically enough from ours as 'insane'; not for our propensity to abuse both animals and humans; not for the indifference with which we destroy most the world so we can then rule over what remains of it, and not for the duplicity with which we whitewash the resulting horror, crowing that we have now 'saved the future'. This, then, becomes the film's Big Question: do we *want* such a future? In Drew Goddard's *The Cabin in the Woods* (2012), two dying teenagers answer it: a world in which humans are capable of the deliberate slaughter of others, even in the 'cause' of human survival, is not worth saving. Apocalypse now, they say. Out with humanity, they say. 'It's time to give someone else a chance.'[84] *12 Monkeys*, conversely, refuses to answer the question, instead throwing it into the viewer's lap.

If time is not linear, then the future is predetermined. But even in a deterministic universe, we can still exercise our free will: not to change the future, but certainly to give our 'reading of the whole thing'. We can look at the devastation of others and the skimpy reasons that excuse it, and we can condone or condemn, accept or reject. We may not be able to save the future, but at least we can decide how many shreds of human dignity we would like to preserve as we face it.

Footnotes

73. Ashbrook, *The Pocket Essential Terry Gilliam*, p. 72.
74. Marks, *Terry Gilliam*, p. 167.
75. Marks, *Terry Gilliam*, p. 158.
76. Del Rio, 'The Remaking', p. 395.
77. Gilliam, *Gilliamesque*, p. 239.
78. The exchange is quoted in Stubbs, 'Dreams', pp. 121-2.
79. Gilliam in Christie, *Gilliam on Gilliam*, p. 228.
80. Lashmet, '"The Future is History"', p. 62.
81. Fry and Craig, 'A Carnival of Apes', p. 11.
82. Marks, *Terry Gilliam*, p. 167.
83. ibid.
84. Goddard, *The Cabin in the Woods* (2012).

8. More *Monkeys*: The TV series

'But what if you could take it back? All of it? A reset switch? You'd hit it, right?' This is the Cosmic Carrot dangled in front of viewers via voice-over in Season 1, Episode 1 of *12 Monkeys* for TV (2015-18). Indeed, the entire series is based on the premise that you *can* take it back, all of it, and the content of the 26 episodes of the first two seasons (of a total of 47 episodes stretched over four seasons) can be boiled down to one single sentence: someone, somewhere, is always hitting the reset switch.

Terry Matalas and Travis Fickett, the series' creators, originally conceived of it simply as a time travelling show with no relation to Gilliam's film. They took their script for the pilot of what was then called *Splinter* to Atlas Entertainment, the producers of the film. Atlas had been wanting to make a TV series based on the film for some time, and so *Splinter* became *12 Monkeys* for TV. Gilliam was neither told nor consulted and less than delighted when he found out. 'I know nothing about that', he said when asked about his involvement with the show. 'That's just ridiculous. It doesn't have anything to do with me and no-one has contacted me. It's a very dumb idea. That's what I think.'[85]

Indeed, most of the movie's smart ideas went straight out of the window. The series starts out by ripping off the film's basic plot: a virus wipes out the planet's population; a team of scientists from the future send a man back in time to fix it all; he falls for a scientist from that time who has managed to send a garbled warning about the virus's origin to the future. Many of the original film's characters are taken over, modified to fit the series format and its more basic ideas. Never worried about making the subtly implied painfully obvious, the TV series turns Kathryn Railly into Cassandra Railly (played by Amanda Schull). Brad Pitt's manic Jeffrey Goines undergoes a sex change to reappear as Jennifer Goines (Emily Hampshire). The film's lead scientist Jones and (presumably) the cartoon-character Professor Grozenschiffer amalgamate into Dr. Katarina Jones née Werner (Barbara Sukowa), characterised mostly by her heavy German accent and unintelligible mutterings about time paradoxes and causality. The apocalypse is moved from 1996 to 2017; the rescue attempt from 2035 to 2043, and the Army of the 12 Monkeys, a red herring in Gilliam's film, becomes the real threat. Cole's death at the airport, the original film's most traumatic scene and driver of its plot, is unceremoniously deleted, and with it most of the sense of hopelessness that distinguishes the thoughtful, measured and doom-laden original from its relentlessly action-packed, hectically paced, and ever-optimistic copycat.

Of the show's four seasons, only the first two, aired in 2015 and 2016 respectively, are of interest in this context. Season 3 (2017) retained too few links to the original film to make it relevant for discussion here (as per the triumphant announcement of Season 3: '12 Monkeys is Back, and It's Abandoned the Movie For Good');[86] Season 4 (2018) had not yet aired at the time of this writing. The first two seasons essentially rely on three basic premises, which I will take in turn below. The first is the most elementary assumption of your average time travel movie: time is linear, and since the future follows on the past, you *can* go back and fix it all. The second is the central theme of the moralistic drama, namely the ethical struggle between personal motives and the Greater Good, which in the series replaces the original film's implicit discussion of free will and predestination. The third is the most basic cliché of the action flick: it presumes that absolutely everything—events, concepts, even cosmic processes like Time—can be simplified and personified. Once it has a human face, you can deal with it *mano a mano*, and saving the world becomes a whole lot simpler, at least conceptually speaking. For what is required in this noble cause is not intellect, conceptualisation, compassion or reflection, but simply a certain level of technology and a man of action who can kick Time's butt.

Pushing the Reset Button: Rinse and Repeat

The idea that you can go back and fix it all naturally implies linear time. 'If you break the past, the future follows', Cole (Aaron Stanford) informs us in Season 1, Episode 1 (S1E1): all you have to do to arrive at a future you like better is to go back to the requisite moment in the past, find the reset button, and push it. 'They found something: a possible re-set switch', Cole tells Railly as he tries to recruit her (S1E1). 'Something started in your time, finished in mine. The last resort. Our only option is to undo it. Stop the plague from ever happening in the first place.' In linear time, this will create an alternate reality, resulting in the erasure of the entire timeline from which Cole was sent and thus also in Cole's death. But Cole doesn't mind: nothing in his world, he says, is worth preserving. 'It'll be rewritten into something better', he tells Railly with that indomitable optimism of the Hollywood action hero. The proof of success would be his own disappearance: if Cole pushes the reset button and is still around a second later, he knows his mission has failed, and sets off gamely in search of a different button.

TV *12 Monkeys* is also fatally addicted to another Hollywood cliché: the One Man Syndrome. Just as only One Man can fix it (the onus here is squarely on Cole, with helping hands belonging to Railly, Jones, his friend Ramse, and Jennifer), One Man is responsible for the End of the World. Forget complex causes like environmental devastation, man-made disasters or a collective abdication of responsibility. The solution is simple: find the One Man at fault and kill him. Series format mandates that the pot be kept boiling, which means that this formula must fail again and again. Each time it does, the show pays lip service to the idea that it ain't that simple, but then, failing to come up with anything more complex, merely recycles the recipe.

In S1E1, Cole goes back in time to assassinate Leland Goines, the originator of the virus, to prevent its release. He manages to kill Goines, but then realises that he has not managed to rewrite the future because he does not disappear himself. By the end of Season 2, we are no further along in our thinking—it's still One Man who is responsible for it all. 'What if we could find the one responsible? The Witness?', asks Railly in S2E8. Thus, the series is stuck in a plot loop consisting predominantly of chases, killings, and attempts on people's lives. The Time Travel Team (Cole, Railly, Jones and assorted minor characters) try to kill the Bad Guys responsible for the apocalypse; the Bad Guys try to bring about the apocalypse by killing people called the 'Primaries' who have a special link to Time Itself and whose murder causes a time paradox. As Railly once put it in an unintentional indictment of the series' blueprint, it's basically 'rinse and repeat' (S1E10). Innovation amounts to going back to a different year, thinking you've finally hit the right button (landed in the right time and killed the right guy), finding out you didn't, and picking a different year. In S2E10, the grand idea is to go back to 1957 and prevent the last Primary from being paradoxed. 'And you're sure that'll stop all this?', Railly asks Jones hopefully. Jones is sure, but of course she's wrong. In S2E11, we are bored with the same hopeful dialogue: 'You're sure this will work, right?', asks Cole. 'We stop the paradox, we fix Time?' Rinse, repeat. On some occasions the formulaic plot does yield practical benefits, offering considerable scope for costume changes (Cassandra gets to dress to impress in 1944, 1957, the 1980s, and so forth) and for recycling existing footage as flashbacks. On other occasions it masquerades as philosophical insight, as in this speech by Cole in S2E3:

> I was sent back in time to kill a man. That was supposed to fix everything. It didn't. So I killed more people. Nothing changed. And then I saved someone. Someone who should have died. And that—that is what changed things. It's the only thing that's ever made any difference.

Unlike Gilliam's film, then, the show is not about physics or philosophy, art or science, but about morality.

The idea that the world can be saved ought to create a sense of urgency and personal investment in the heroes who are trying to save it. It doesn't. Part of the attraction of Gilliam's film resides in the unavoidable sympathy aroused by the figure of Cole, a perennially vulnerable, naked, leaking, confused and exploited man who learns to love life and is then 'volunteered' for sacrifice. TV *12 Monkeys* not only replaces him with a bog-standard action hero but also deletes the inevitability of death. *Everyone in the show dies all the time*: Ramse and Jones (S1E4); Railly and Cole (S2E3); Jones again (S1E6 and S2E11); Railly again (S1E9), and Jennifer Goines (S2E11). But it's okay because we always get to go back in time to reverse these deaths. If not, as happens with Jennifer Goines, just replace the dead character with her younger self (this scene in S2E11 yields one of the show's few funny lines, when Old/Dying Jennifer encounters her younger nonplussed self: 'Hello, egg. I'm chicken'). Essentially, the series sacrifices audience identification with characters to action. With all these deaths, first endured and then erased, all of it loses meaning: life, death, even apocalypse.

The second season ends with a guest appearance by Madeleine Stowe, the original Railly, who introduces Cole to a new kind of time travel of the mind. Forget the time machine, she says. 'Drink me', she tells him as she pushes some red leaves into Cole's hand, which will take his mind back to any timeline he's visited before. But even this Alice in Wonderland scene does not represent a true novelty. There is no change in objective, only in transportation method. The goal is still what it ever was: 'Find you in 1957, take control, undo your mistakes, stop the paradox, and save us all' (S2E13). 'Rinse and repeat' does not get more sophisticated in the repetition, or because the line is delivered by the otherwise incomparable Madeleine Stowe.

Motives and Morals: Everything is Personal

In fairness, it has to be said that the series does not focus exclusively on the question of how to save the world, but also spends some time on the far more interesting question of why one should bother. Here again, however, much of the potential for profundity is deleted from the outset. There is no Sartrean paradox here, no hidden *Huis Clos* (even given a second chance, is it actually possible to 'undo your mistakes'?). What little consideration of the free will versus determinism dilemma there is remains cursory at best, flailing around helplessly at plot- and statement level. The reason for this flatness is simple: all motives for either wanting to save the world or destroy it are purely personal. In fact, they are usually identical: love for a person who would die either in the pre- or post-apocalypse world. The various motives of different characters are briefly related in a series of background stories, perhaps conceived of as a way of reinjecting some interest into characters who can die in any episode and whose deaths don't matter because we know they'll be back in the next. Whatever the reason, these stories are more likely to make characters appear petty rather than conflicted.

The question that recurs in these stories and that the show apparently asks us to take seriously, rather than dismissing it outright as an ethical absurdity, is whether it's okay to kill seven billion people to save one person you love. It is seriously debated between Railly and her (on again/off again/finally ex-) boyfriend Aaron (Noah Bean) in S1E10. Gradually it emerges that every last one of our heroes (with whom we're nevertheless supposed to identify) has his or her personal little motive for either wanting to prevent Armageddon or wanting it to go ahead. As Cole confesses to Railly in S1E5, he is consumed with guilt because he killed two kindly old folks for food and shelter and was forgiven by the old woman as she was dying. This is why he wants to 'fix' the apocalypse: if Time resets, he will be erased, along with his entire timeline. Charitable viewers might call it atonement, but the scheme does carry the strong whiff of a rather smug suicide. In fact, Cole's friend Ramse (the re-boot of the original's Jose, played here by Kirk Acevedo) accuses him directly of merely wanting to delete himself rather than save the world (S1E5).

For his part, Ramse wants Armageddon to go ahead because he wants to save his son, who, born in the post-apocalyptic timeline, will be erased if the world is saved. Conversely-yet-similarly, Jones wants to reverse Armageddon not to save the world but her daughter, who died of the plague. Jennifer wants to end the world because she's in love with Cole ('Why do I always have to do bad things to get your attention?', she whines at him in S2E2) and because she is told that if she destroys the world the voices in her head will stop (S2E2). Aaron is happy for everyone on Earth to perish in the plague so long as he survives it with Railly. 'You save the people that you love', he tells Railly when she begs him to help her prevent the apocalypse. 'And that's what matters, right?' (S1E12). Given the choice between preventing Armageddon and riding it out in a bunker somewhere, just you and the one or two people you care about, people are usually perfectly happy to say 'To hell with everyone else'. Cole and Ramse regularly debate the 'morality' of sacrificing billions to save the one you love. 'Is that what you've become?', Cole accuses Ramse, 'Someone who would kill seven billion to save just one?' Ramse retorts angrily: 'You'd do the same thing' (S1E13). The series even indulges in shouting matches about whose egotism is more justifiable. 'My selfishness was in line with saving billions of lives', Jones rants at Ramse (S2E3). 'Yours was bent to destroy them!' Everyone in the show is in business for themselves, wanting to either cause or prevent the apocalypse to service their personal traumas (cue Jennifer in S1E11: 'I want to be a daughter again'). Selfish desires, like the original Cole's heart-breaking wish to live in a dying world, no longer result in inner conflict, like the one endured by both Cole and Railly in the film. On the contrary, none of the 'I'm-a-better-egoist-than-you'-slinging matches in the series ever result in any of its characters stopping to question their own motives. Unlike his namesake in Gilliam's film, TV-Cole is profoundly unconflicted; he is on mission, never hesitating, all the time.

Perhaps the one thing that the series has in common with Gilliam's film is the insight that it is not and has never been about saving the world, merely about serving various degrees of self-interest. The film presents this to us as the most appalling reality imaginable; the series sugarcoats it, sweetening the bitter pill with the language of love—Jennifer's for Cole; Cole's for Railly; Aaron's for Railly; Jones's for her daughter; Ramse's for his son. 'The only world I ever gave a damn about was the one with you in it', Cole tells Railly (S2E8). Only in a preposterously egotistical universe could this pass for a romantic statement.

Killing Time: Everything is Personified

TV *12 Monkeys* practically teems with mysterious semi-metaphysical characters. An evil Pallid Man makes his first appearance in S1E3. The mission of a character named the Witness is withheld for long episodes until it is revealed that he seeks to destroy Time Itself. There is the Army of the 12 Monkeys, a conglomerate bent on the same evil purpose. There are so-called Primaries, described as the 'living, breathing gears in Time's wristwatch' (S2E4). Their special relationship with Time keeps Time moving and in sync, just as their destruction causes time paradoxes and threatens to unravel Time Itself. There are the Messengers who, out to destroy Time, are in the business of murdering Primaries (or 'paradoxing' them, in the show's parlance) one by one. There are the Scavengers, led by an initially evil guy called Deacon (Todd Stashwick) who later turns out to have his moments. There are the Daughters, led by Jennifer, who seem to serve no purpose in the show beyond providing Jennifer, after the failure of her initial quest to end the world, with a new purpose in life. There is the Mother, a cult figure of the Destroyers of Time. This figure, it turns out in a major plot twist, is Cassandra Railly, whose son born to her and Cole—two time travellers outside of their own time—is fêted as the 'Child out of Time' in an assembly of hooded Messengers that looks every bit like a chapter meeting of the KKK (S2E13). And there are assorted scavengers, Nazi war criminals and Mossad agents.

We might read this bewildering palette of myth-laden individuals and groups as a rather simplistic way of dealing with one of the original film's most central themes: the question of free will versus determinism. One of the clearest signs of this is the personification of Time, sometimes also known as Fate, which—or rather, who—

emerges as perhaps the most significant character of the series. 'I am Time', Jennifer announces solemnly (S2E2), by which she means that she's the Primary Patient. But Time is anthropomorphised by others as well. 'Time is cruel, Mr. Cole', Jones warns. 'Believe me: I've learned enough about Time to fear it. And so should you' (S1E2). Later she tells him that repeated time travel will eventually kill him because 'Time takes what it's owed' (S1E6). The personification of Time is meant to be taken quite literally; Time, we are told, is a conscious entity that needs Primaries to think (S2E8). The series is full of endless talk about what Time wants and what it doesn't, what it 'likes' and what it doesn't, and above all what it needs: 'Time needs you to set things right, to fix it, to stop the 12 Monkeys from destroying the world' (S2E8). If Time is a person, it can be killed, which is the primary goal of the 12 Monkeys, the Messengers, the Witness and assorted Nazis. Rather late in Season 2 we're finally furnished with a motive: the Witness tells Railly that he wants to destroy Time so there's no more death, which sounds good to Railly until Jennifer convinces her that death is 'a time clock that makes us better. Makes us love harder' (S2E6). Lest we dismiss this as the metaphysical mumbo-jumbo typical for the show, there is an actual point to this. Personalising Time is the series' way of sneaking agency in through the back door. Turning processes into people—the Pallid Man, the Witness, the Messengers, Time Itself—implies that someone is doing this, and if someone is doing it, someone else might prevent it.

The reason this matters is that it goes right to the heart of the free will versus determinism dilemma. In fact, the series has garnered some critical accolades for its 'deep philosophical meditation on the concept of predestination versus free will'.[87] In reality, TV *12 Monkeys*' take on the matter is about as shallow and unphilosophical as it gets: both positions are simply assigned a moral value. The Bad Guys are generally adherents of determinism, believing that the future is set. 'All of this is preordained, scripted by Time, unmovable, because there is nothing more powerful than Fate', they intone ominously (S1E13). At the outset of Season 2, a voice-over explains to us why Cole and Railly have consistently failed to stop the plague: 'Fate was not on their side.' 'If something was meant to be, it shall be', the Messenger tells Jones (S2E1). The good guys, conversely, are great believers in human agency and free will. Convinced that 'there's no such thing as Fate' (Railly in S2E3), good guys gamely rinse and repeat whenever yet another attempt to prevent the plague or save Time has failed. So unwavering is their belief in human agency that they even fail to distinguish between freedom of will and freedom of action. Accordingly, both are constantly confused with each other, even declared to be the same. 'What needs to be done to save the world is to believe you can' (Jones to Cole in S2E8). 'There are many endings. The right one is the one that you choose' (Jones to Cole in S2E9). No rationale is ever offered in support of either free will or determinism. Both remain statements untethered from any philosophical context and unsupported by any argument, propped up by nothing beyond the moral underpinning of the characters making them.

Once free will has morphed from a philosophical to a moral position, the series has obviously committed itself to advocating human agency and its ability to change the world. The primary engines of this worldview are the personalisation of concepts and One-Manism. Things in the series go wrong not because cosmic processes are at work or because humanity in general has failed to address calamitous developments from global warming to irresponsible science, but because of One Man (or Woman). Equally implausibly, things in the series sometimes go right because One Man (or Woman) stands in the way of Evil. In S2E7, the Witness takes control of Railly to sabotage the time machine. See?, the show tells us, it's all about agency. In S2E10, the evil Nazi doctor, under the watchful eye of the Witness, creates the first Messenger. If we can only destroy that prototype, the conclusion is, we'll have fixed Time, leaving only the plague to be dealt with. In S2E11, we're faced with the same logic in reverse: the Good Guys' plan here is to kill the Witness, which will fix the plague, and then, at some later date, to worry about the fact that Time is coming apart at the seams. In S2E8, the Bad Guys try to kill Jones to prevent the invention of the time machine in 2020. Their reasoning is identical to Good Guy logic: it's always about *one* person. Nothing this person has ever thought, apparently, can possibly be thought by anyone else. Thoughts can be unthought, inventions uncreated, by killing this *one* person. Without Jones, time travel will never be invented.

Bizarrely for a time travel show, TV *12 Monkeys* removes the principal mechanism that describes reality—cause and effect—entirely from the cosmological realm and transfers it to the personal. That gives it leave to delete the original film's reflexiveness, inner struggles and painful dilemmas, replacing it all with mere action and characters defined by it, action heroes and anti-heroes. Bad Guys try to kill Time; Good Guys try to fix it (Figure 9). Rinse, repeat.

Figure 9: We'll fix you, Time: action heroes Cole (Aaron Stanford) and Cassandra Railly (Amanda Schull) in 12 Monkeys for TV (Season 4, 2018)

Terry Matalas, co-creator of the series, has defined its attitude toward time, free will and determinism, and its differences from its precursor films, in precisely these terms:

> Ultimately, our version of predestination—and where it diverges from *La Jetée* or the original film—is that it's a basically a bullfight, a ballet, against Time. That Time is something to be wrestled with and fought against—and after you've bled and been beaten and gotten your ass thoroughly kicked, *maybe* you've moved it an inch. The idea of a closed loop works beautifully in a film, but for the story and the emotion of a TV series to really resonate, the characters and the audience have to believe that change is possible. It's hard-fought and not without causalities along the way, but we've already seen that time *can* be affected. Whether it can be changed *enough*—or how Time might account for those changes—are some of the central questions of the show.[88]

Good Guys fight hard, they bleed and are beaten, they get their asses kicked. The frustration of just *maybe* moving an inch after all these 'causalities' (did Matalas mean 'casualties' here?) is cheerfully endured because good guys are steadfast in their belief that change is possible (there's that indomitable American spirit again, familiar from every apocalypse movie and every action flick). Time is not a neutral process that cares nothing about whether we believe it to be linear, circular or loopy, but a person—in fact, it is the principal adversary 'to be wrestled with and fought against'. What we have here is not a sci-fi series involving time travel (which would have to take time as a concept a great deal more seriously), much less, in the words of that generous critic, a 'deep philosophical meditation on the concept of predestination versus free will'. Instead, the show turns its back firmly not only on its precursor films, but also on philosophy and science (as well as culture and history: none of Gilliam's wonderful intertextuality with cultural artefacts, from films to lectures to poetry to paintings, made it into the show). Philosophical concepts like free will and determinism, cosmological concepts like time, drown in a mix of technobabble, murder scenes and costume changes. Closer to *Die Hard* than the original *12 Monkeys*, the series replaces thought with action.

Action without thought, however, is a woefully inadequate response to either concept or catastrophe. This is the simplest reason why the series never goes anywhere, or rather why it ends up in the same place all the time. Caught in the eternal plot loop, it can only rinse and repeat. In its obsession with seat-of-the-pants plot twists, edge-of-the-seat chases and skin-of-the-teeth escapes, the series does achieve extra-diegetically what its bad guys attempt to do diegetically: it kills time. But it does not take time seriously, just as it does not think seriously about free will or determinism. The last *12 Monkeys* that did that dates back to 1995. For the series, trapped in its belief that you have to kick ass to move an inch, that ideas are people, and that your choices are limited to either fixing time or killing it, there is no going back.

Footnotes

85. Gilliam in an interview with *ScreenDaily*, quoted by Hatfull, '12 Monkeys TV Show.'
86. See Anders, '*12 Monkeys* is Back.'
87. Seghers, '12 Monkeys: Season 1 Review.'
88. Matalas is quoted in Lovick, 'The Power of a Paradox.'

9. Coda: Gilliam's Art of the Possible

One of Gilliam's greatest fears as a film-maker seems to be getting caught in a loop much like the one that characterises the *12 Monkeys* series, to become derivative, repetitive. 'The idea of simple replication has never really interested me', he wrote in his memoirs.[89] This is why he famously refused to read Orwell's *1984* before making *Brazil*, and why he refused to see *La Jetée* before making *12 Monkeys*. What is most interesting about his quest for originality, though, is that he describes it in temporal terms, and the timeline he conjures up is *not* linear:

> This way I can be confident I haven't ripped anybody off, because what I've done is actually based on a pre-emptive foretaste, a recollection from the future—the memory I will have of these things once I've finally got round to reading or watching them.

> If I choose to base what I'm doing at any given moment on the way I think I will remember having felt in ten years' time, who's to stop me?[90]

Anticipated memory; recollections from the future, pre-emptive foretastes of the as-yet-unknown. Just as in Einstein's non-linear spacetime, just as in Railly's recognition of a Cole she sees for the first time in her life, Terry Gilliam's creative universe is a space where timelines merge. Memory is untethered from the past; pre-emption is unmoored from the future ('I think I *will* remember *having felt* in ten years' time'). This kind of four-dimensional creativity is enabled by two basic steps: by a rejection of linearity—such as defines the relationship between past, present and future, or that between original and replication—and by a partiality for the possible over the real. 'I much prefer to refer to my probably inaccurate idea of something than the actuality of the thing itself', says Gilliam.[91]

This, then, is the most principal difference between *12 Monkeys* the film and *12 Monkeys* the show: one displays a profound fondness for (possibly inaccurate) ideas, the other an unwavering dedication to 'actuality' in the form of action. One posits that humans, while unfree in actuality, can find freedom in ideas, even if these ideas remain theoretical, like the film's beautiful landscapes, songs and poems; and even if they can never be realised, like Cole's and Railly's failed attempt to smell the flowers before Doomsday. The other proposes that freedom of will is the same as freedom of action, but renders freedom of will irrelevant by endlessly spinning its wheels in useless actions that end up applying the same failed remedies to the same old wounds. One is defined by its ideas, the other by its format—the 'actuality of the thing itself' mandates 'simple replication' of the same plot.

Gilliam's film, that spectacular mess and prime example of the Art of the Possible, will most likely inspire passionate discussion, wondrous bemusement, confused questions and violent disagreements long after, on TV, the last time-trip has been taken, the last Primary paradoxed, and the final Messenger killed. Because this is, in the end, the great advantage of Gilliam's Art of the Possible over the Art of Actuality: it may not kick Time's ass, but it does stand up to it.

Footnotes

89. Gilliam, *Gilliamesque*, p. 264.
90. ibid.
91. ibid.

Bibliography/Filmography

12 Monkeys. TV-series. Created by Terry Matalas and Travis Fickett (Universal / SyFy 2015-18).

Aldersey-Williams, Hugh. 'Terry Gilliam: Through a Lens Weirdly.' *Graphis* 316 (July/August 1998): 96-101.

Anders, Charlie Jane. '*12 Monkeys* is Back, and It's Abandoned the Movie for Good.' *Culture* (19 May 2017). https://www.wired.com/2017/05/12-monkeys-tv-review/

Andress, Justin. '"12 Monkeys" Showrunner Terry Matalas Talks Season 3, Fate, and Ratings.' *Inverse* (25 May 2016). https://www.inverse.com/article/16107-12-monkeys-showrunner-terry-matalas-talks-season-3-fate-and-ratings

'Are Space and Time an Illusion? Space Time.' PBS Digital Studios. https://www.youtube.com/watch?v=YycAzdtUIko.

Ashbrook, John. *The Pocket Essential Terry Gilliam.* Harpenden: Pocket Essentials, 2000.

Baer, John, James C. Kaufman, and Roy F. Baumeister. *Are We Free? Psychology and Free Will.* Oxford, New York: Oxford UP, 2008.

Barr, Merrill. 'NYCC Exclusive: "12 Monkeys" Executive Producer Terry Matalas on Season 2 and Show's Roots.' *Forbes Media and Entertainment* (9 October 2015). https://www.forbes.com/sites/merrillbarr/2015/10/09/12-monkeys-season-2-nycc-terry-matalas/3/#5ff313d91774

Baumeister, Roy F., E. J. Masicampo, and C. Nathan DeWall. 'Prosocial Benefits of Feeling Free: Disbelief in Free Will Increases Aggression and Reduces Helpfulness.' *Personality and Social Psychology Bulletin* 35/2 (2009): 260-8.

Bergson, Henri. *Time and Free Will.* Trans. F. L. Pogson. London: George Allen & Unwin, 1959.

Blumenau, Ralph. 'Free Will & Predestination.' *Philosophy Now* 20 (Spring 1998): 20-2.

Calhoun, John. '12 Monkeys.' *Theatre Crafts International* 30/3 (March 1996): 34-7.

Canavan, Gerry. '"You can't change anything": Freedom and Control in *Twelve Monkeys.*' *The Cinema of Terry Gilliam: it's a mad world.* Ed. Jeff Birkenstein, Anna Froula and Karen Randell. Brighton/New York: Wallflower Press, 2013. 92-103.

Cartwright, Mark. 'The Aztec Calendar.' *Ancient History Encyclopedia* (25 April 2016). https://www.ancient.eu/article/896/

Caruso, Gregg D. *Free Will and Consciousness: A Determinist Account of the Illusion of Free Will.* Lanham, MD: Lexington Books, 2012.

Channel 4 Film Review of *12 Monkeys. Rotten Tomatoes* (27 May 2011). https://www.rottentomatoes.com/m/12_monkeys/

Charity, Tom. 'Monkey Puzzle.' *Time Out* 1338 (10-17 April 1996): 18-20.

Christie, Ian (ed.). *Gilliam on Gilliam.* London, New York: Faber and Faber, 1999.

Craig, J. Robert. 'Trapping Simians in the Scottish Highlands: A Viewer Response to the Hitchcock MacGuffin in Terry Gilliam's *12 Monkeys*.' *Journal of Evolutionary Psychology* XIX 3/4 (August 1998): 244-9.

Cridland, Sean. 'In the Twinkling of an Eye: Nietzschean Undercurrents in Terry Gilliam's *12 Monkeys*.' *Film and Philosophy* 3 (1996): 130-7.

Del Rio, Elena. 'The Remaking of *La Jetée*'s Time-Travel Narrative: *Twelve Monkeys* and the Rhetoric of Absolute Visibility.' *Science Fiction Studies* 28 (2001): 383-98.

Dirks, Tim. 'The History of Film: The 1990s.' *AMC Filmsite*. http://www.filmsite.org/90sintro.html

Einstein, Albert. *Relativity: The Special and the General Theory. A Popular Exposition*. Trans. Robert W. Lawson. London: Methuen, 1920.

Eller, Claudia. 'Average Cost of Making, Marketing Movie Soars.' *Los Angeles Times* (8 March 1995). http://articles.latimes.com/1995-03-08/business/fi-40252_1_average-cost

Emmerich, Roland (dir.). *Independence Day*. Feature Film (Twentieth Century Fox 1996).

Faunce, B. K. 'Paranoia and Spectatorship in *12 Monkeys*.' *The Psychoanalytic Review* 84/3 (June 1997): 453-9.

Foote, Bud. *The Connecticut Yankee in the Twentieth Century: Travels to the Past in Science Fiction*. New York: Greenwood P, 1991.

Foucault, Michel. *Discipline and Punish: The Birth of the Prison*. Trans. Alan Sheridan. New York: Vintage, 1979.

Fountain, Nigel. 'Monkey Business.' *Terry Gilliam: Interviews*. Ed. David Sterritt and Lucille Rhodes. Jackson: UP of Mississippi, 2004. 107-12.

Fowler, Matt, and Eric Goldman. 'Everything You Need to Know About SyFy's 12 Monkeys.' *Fallout 76* (15 January 2015). http://uk.ign.com/articles/2015/01/16/everything-you-need-to-know-about-syfys-12-monkeys

Fried, John. '12 Monkeys.' *Cineaste* 22/3 (1996): 47-8.

Fry, Carrol, and J. Robert Craig. 'A Carnival of Apes: A Bakhtinian Perspective on *Twelve Monkeys*.' *Journal of the Fantastic in the Arts* 13/1 (2002): 3-12.

Fuchs, Cynthia. 'The Monkey's Man' / '12 Monkeys.' *Philadelphia City Paper* (5 January 1996): 16-18, 50-51.

Gilliam, Terry. *Gilliamesque: My Me, Me, Me Memoir*. Edinburgh, London: Canongate, 2015.

Gilliam, Terry (dir.). *12 Monkeys: The Future is History*. Feature Film (Universal City Studios 1995).

Goddard, Drew (dir.). *The Cabin in the Woods*. Feature Film (Lionsgate 2012).

Goldman, Eric. '12 Monkeys Cast and EP Talk Season 3's New Eras and New Binge-Ready Schedule.' *ING* (17 May 2017). http://uk.ign.com/articles/2017/05/17/12-monkeys-cast-and-ep-talk-season-3s-new-eras-and-new-binge-ready-schedule

Greenberg, Harvey Roy. '12 Monkeys: The Rags of Time.' *Film and Philosophy* 3 (1996): 123-9.

Hand, Elizabeth. *12 Monkeys: The Future is History*. New York: Harper-Collins, 1995.

Hatfull, Jonathan. '12 Monkeys TV Show "A Very Dumb Idea" Says Terry Gilliam.' *SciFiNow* (4 September 2013). https://www.scifinow.co.uk/news/12-monkeys-tv-show-a-very-dumb-idea-says-terry-gilliam/

Hawking, Stephen. *A Brief History of Time*. London, New York: Bantam P, 1998.

Heidegger, Martin. *Being and Time*. Trans. John Macquarrie and Edward Robinson. San Francisco: Harper, 1962.

Jackson, Mick (dir.). *Volcano*. Feature Film (Twentieth Century Fox 1997).

James, Nick. 'Time and the Machine.' *Terry Gilliam: Interviews*. Ed. David Sterritt and Lucille Rhodes Jackson: UP of Mississippi, 2004. 113-6.

Kane, Robert. *A Contemporary Introduction to Free Will*. Oxford, New York: Oxford UP, 2005.

Kane, Robert. *The Significance of Free Will*. Oxford, New York: Oxford UP, 1998.

Klawans, Stuart. 'A Dialogue with Terry Gilliam.' *Terry Gilliam: Interviews*. Ed. David Sterritt and Lucille Rhodes Jackson: UP of Mississippi, 2004. 141-69.

Lashmet, David. '"The Future is History": *12 Monkeys* and the Origin of AIDS.' *Mosaic: a journal for the interdisciplinary study of literature* 33/4 (December 2000): 55-72.

Legare, Michael Joseph. 'The Question of Free Will.' *When Things Seem Odd: Polly and the Internal Guardian*. Victoria, B.C.: Friesen P, 2016. 262-95.

Levy, Emanuel. 'Review of *12 Monkeys*.' *Compact Variety: The Ultimate Entertainment Resource Guide* 1/2 (December 22, 1995).

Lovick, Jennifer. 'The Power of a Paradox: A Lesson About Time Travel from SyFy's 12 Monkeys (Part I).' *Signal Noise Magazine* (30 June 2016). http://www.signaltonoisemag.com/allarticles/2016/6/30/the-power-of-a-paradox-a-lesson-about-time-travel-on-syfys-12-monkeys-part-i

Marker, Chris. *La Jetée: The Book Version of the Legendary (1964) Science Fiction Film*. New York: Zone Books, 1992.

Marker, Chris (dir.). *La Jetée: ciné-roman* (Argos Films 1962).

Marks, Peter. *Terry Gilliam*. Manchester: Manchester UP, 2009.

McCabe, Bob. *Dark Knights & Holy Fools: The Art and Films of Terry Gilliam*. London: Orion, 1999.

McCabe, Joseph. 'Exclusive: Producers Travis Fickett and Terry Matalas on Time Travel, Gender Swapping, and SyFy's 12 Monkeys.' *Nerdist* (17 January 2015). https://nerdist.com/exclusive-producers-travis-fickett-and-terry-matalas-on-time-travel-gender-swapping-and-syfys-12-monkeys/

McTaggart, John M. E. 'The Unreality of Time.' *Mind* 17 (1908): 457-74.

Mele, Rick. '"12 Monkeys": 10 Things to Know About the SciFi Movie-Turned-TV-Show.' *Huffington Post* (15 January 2015). https://www.huffingtonpost.ca/2015/01/15/12-monkeys-tv-show-syfy-showcase_n_6480078.html?guccounter=1

Morgan, David. 'Extremities.' *Sight and Sound* (January 1996): 18-21.

Morgan, David. 'Filming Twelve Monkeys.' *Wide Angle/Closeup: Conversations with Filmmakers by David Morgan* (1995). http://www.wideanglecloseup.com/monkeys_filming.html

Ng, Philiana. '"12 Monkeys" Producer on Syfy Series: "It's a Complete Reimagining".' *The Hollywood Reporter* (14 July 2014). https://www.hollywoodreporter.com/live-feed/12-monkeys-producer-syfy-series-718532

Nguyen, Hanh. '"12 Monkeys" Season 2: Can the Time Travelers Actually Challenge Fate?' *Hollywood Reporter* (18 April 2016). https://www.hollywoodreporter.com/live-feed/12-monkeys-season-2-884643

Nichols, Shaun, and Joshua Knobe. 'Moral Responsibility and Determinism: The Cognitive Science of Folk Intuitions.' *Noûs* 41/4 (2007): 663-85.

Nietzsche, Friedrich. *Thus Spake Zarathustra*. Trans. R. J. Hollingdale. New York: Penguin, 1969.

Ogden, Sofia K., and Ashley D. Biebers, eds. *Psychology of Denial*. New York: Nova Science, 2010.

Penley, Constance. 'Time Travel, Primal Scene, and the Critical Dystopia.' *Liquid Metal: The Science Fiction Film Reader*. Ed. Sean Redmond. New York: Wallflower P, 2004. 126-35.

Perry, Douglas. 'Simian Deficiencies.' *Cinescape* (July 1996): 66-7.

Pizzello, Stephen. '*Twelve Monkeys*: A Dystopian Trip Through Time.' *American Cinematographer* 77/1 (January 1996): 36-44.

Rafferty, Terrence. 'Time Out Of Joint: The hyperkinetic "12 Monkeys" and a Fascist-era "Richard III."' *The New Yorker* (22 January 1996): 84-7.

Richardson, Conner. 'Twelve Monkeys: Symbols, Lighting, & Camera Angles.' 18 January 2013. https://connerpaige.wordpress.com/2013/01/08/twelve-monkeys-symbols-lighting-camera-angles/

Rosen, Elizabeth K. *Apocalyptic Transformation: Apocalypse and the Postmodern Imagination*. Lanham, MD: Lexington Books, 2008.

Ruben, Matthew. '*12 Monkeys*, postmodernism, and the urban: toward a new method.' *Keyframes: Popular Cinema and Cultural Studies.* Ed. Matthew Tinkcom and Amy Villarejo. London, New York: Routledge, 2001. 312-32.

Schopenhauer, Arthur. *On the Freedom of the Will.* Oxford: Basil Blackwell, 1839.

Seghers, Christine. '12 Monkeys: "Arms of Mine." Review.' *ING* (10 April 2015). http://uk.ign.com/articles/2015/04/11/12-monkeys-arms-of-mine-review

Seghers, Christine. '12 Monkeys: "Lullaby" Review.' *ING* (6 June 2016). http://uk.ign.com/articles/2016/06/07/12-monkeys-lullaby-review

Seghers, Christine. '12 Monkeys: "Paradox" Review.' *ING* (3 April 2015). http://uk.ign.com/articles/2015/04/04/12-monkeys-paradox-review

Seghers, Christine. '12 Monkeys: Season 1 Review.' *IGN* (25 April 2015). http://uk.ign.com/articles/2015/04/25/12-monkeys-season-1-review

Seghers, Christine. '12 Monkeys: Season 3 Review.' *ING* (18 May 2017). http://uk.ign.com/articles/2017/05/18/12-monkeys-season-3-review

Sloma, Christopher. 'Exclusive Q&A with 12 Monkeys TV Series Co-Executive Producer Terry Matalas.' *Daily Dead* (2 February 2015). https://dailydead.com/exclusive-qa-12-monkeys-tv-series-showrunner-terry-matalas/

Spinoza, Benedict de. *Ethics.* Trans. R. H. M. Elwes. Digireads.com (2008).

Stagoll, Cliff. 'Killing Time.' *Philosophy Now* 20 (Spring 1998): 28-30.

Stannard, Russell. *Relativity: A Very Short Introduction.* Oxford: Oxford UP, 2008.

Sterritt, David, and Lucille Rhodes, eds. *Terry Gilliam: Interviews.* Jackson: UP of Mississippi, 2004.

Stinson, Bob. 'Critic Reviews for *Twelve Monkeys* (*12 Monkeys*).' *Rotten Tomatoes.* https://www.rottentomatoes.com/m/12_monkeys/

Stubbs, Phil. 'Dreams.' *Terry Gilliam: Interviews.* Ed. David Sterritt and Lucille Rhodes. Jackson: UP of Mississippi, 2004. 117-23.

Townsend, R. F. *The Aztecs.* London: Thames&Hudson, 2009.

Turl, E. J. *Have We No Choice?* Bognor Regis: New Horizon, 1982.

Velmans, Max. 'How Could Conscious Experiences Affect Brains?' *Journal of Consciousness Studies* 9/11 (2002): 2-29.

Vohs, Kathleen D., and Jonathan W. Schooler. 'The Value of Believing in Free Will: Encouraging a Belief in Determinism Increases Cheating.' *Psychological Science* 19/1 (2008): 49-54.

Wardle, Paul. 'Terry Gilliam.' *Terry Gilliam: Interviews.* Ed. David Sterritt and Lucille Rhodes. Jackson: UP of Mississippi, 2004. 65-106.

Wegner, Daniel. *The Illusion of Conscious Will*. Cambridge: Bradford Books, 2002.

Weishaar, Schuy R. *Masters of the Grotesque: The Cinema of Tim Burton, Terry Gilliam, the Coen Brothers and David Lynch*. Jefferson, N.C.: McFarland, 2012.

Williams, Clifford. *Free Will and Determinism: A Dialogue*. Indianapolis: Hackett, 1980.

Yu, Andy. 'Kant's Argument for Free Will.' *Prometheus Journal* (25 February 2009). http://prometheus-journal.com/2009/02/25/morality-rationality-and-freedom-kant%E2%80%99s-argument-for-free-will/